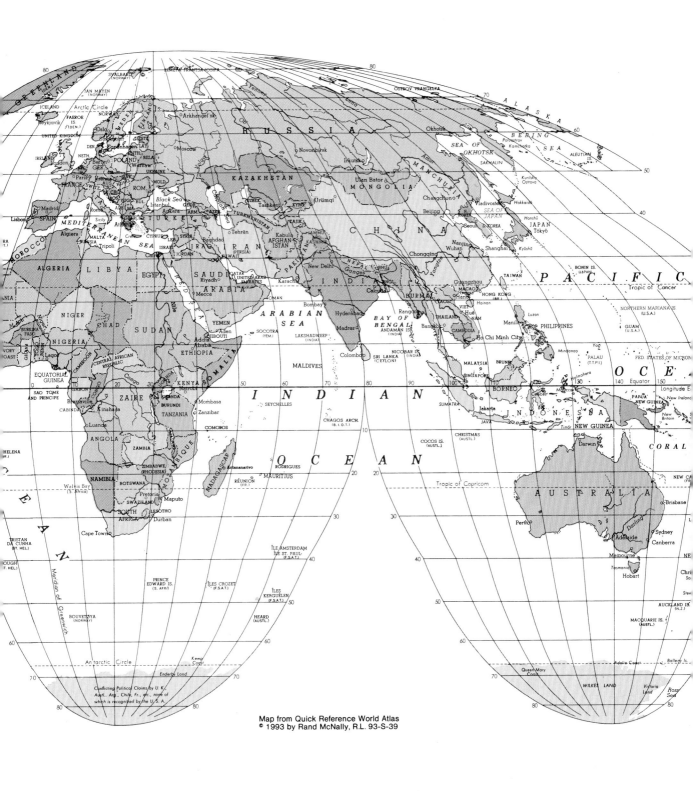

Map from Quick Reference World Atlas
© 1993 by Rand McNally, R.L. 93-S-39

Map from New International Atlas. © 1993 by Rand McNally, R.L. 93-S-39

Enchantment of the World

INDONESIA

By Sylvia McNair

Consultant for Indonesia: Joan D. Winship, M.A., International Education and Training Consultant, Bettendorf, Iowa

Consultant for Reading: Robert L. Hillerich, Ph.D., Professor Emeritus, Bowling Green State University; Consultant, Pinellas County Schools, Florida

CHILDRENS PRESS®
CHICAGO

During a religious festival, women carry offerings of food to the temple.

Library of Congress Cataloging-in-Publication Data

McNair, Sylvia.
    Indonesia / by Sylvia McNair.
        p.   cm. — (Enchantment of the world)
    Includes index.
    Summary: Introduces the geography, people, history,
government, industries, and culture of Indonesia.
    ISBN 0-516-02618-6
    1. Indonesia—Juvenile literature. [1. Indonesia.]
I. Title. II. Series.
DS615.M4   1993   93-3401
SECOND PRINTING, 1994.   CIP
Copyright © 1993 by Childrens Press®, Inc.   AC
All rights reserved. Published simultaneously in Canada.
Printed in the United States of America.
    2 3 4 5 6 7 8 9 10 R 02 01 00 99 98 97 96 95 94

Picture Acknowledgments
AP/Wide World Photos: 54, 55, 56, 58, 60, 61, 63, 65, 69
Culver Pictures: 16, 44, 47 (2 photos), 49
© **John Elk III:** 42, 97
© **Lee Foster:** 36, 85, 90 (left), 104, 105 (left)
GeoIMAGERY: © **Hermine Dreyfuss,** 6 (top left), 18
(right), 29, 78, 83, 84 (top), 90 (right), 91 (2 photos), 92
(2 photos)
H. Armstrong Roberts: © **Damm/Zefa,** 6 (bottom)
Embassy of the Republic of Indonesia: 9
Impact Visuals: © **Joel Crawford,** 68
© **Bonnie Kamin:** 24 (bottom right), 84 (bottom right)
© **Sylvia McNair:** 31 (left)

Odyssey/Frerck/Chicago: © **Robert Frerck,** 5, 6 (top
right), 30 (right), 84 (bottom left), 101 (left)
Photri: 12, 18 (left), 20 (right), 26 (right), 73 (right), 74, 75,
77, 87, 102, 110; © **Aby,** Cover
© **Porterfield/Chickering:** Cover Inset, 28 (right), 86, 94
(bottom), 96 (2 photos), 103, 105 (right), 106 (right)
© **Edward S. Ross:** 19 (right)
Jeff Rotman Photography: © **Jeffrey L. Rotman,** 22
(2 photos)
Bob & Ira Spring: 21 (bottom right), 28 (left), 38 (right), 39
(right), 72, 73 (left), 80 (2 photos), 81, 88 (top), 94 (top),
106 (left)
Tom Stack & Associates: © **Anna E. Zuckerman,** 10, 24
(top); © **Gary Milburn,** 24 (bottom left); © **Manfred
Gottschalk,** 39 (left), 98, 101 (right); © **Inga Spence,** 76;
© **Mike Severns,** 127
Stock Montage: 51
Tony Stone Images: © **Gary Brettnacher,** 15; © **David
Austen,** 34; © **Paul Chesley,** 43; © **Hilarie Kavanagh,** 70;
© **Murray & Associates,** 99
SuperStock International, Inc.: © **J. Day,** 13; © **Alan Brier,**
19 (left); © **K. Scholz,** 38 (left); © **P. Schmid,** 82; © **S.
Vidler,** 100; © **Schuster,** 107
Travel Stock: © **Buddy Mays,** 4, 21 (top right), 30 (left), 31
(right), 107 (right)
Valan: © **John Cancalosi,** 20 (left); © **Robert C. Simpson,**
21 (left); © **Y.R. Tymstra,** 26 (left)
Len W. Meents: Maps on 10, 14, 36
**Courtesy Flag Research Center, Winchester,
Massachusetts 01890:** Flag on back cover
Cover: Ulon Danau Beratan temple in Bedugul
Cover Inset: LeLong dancer

Close-up of sculpture on the Sangeh Temple in Bali

TABLE OF CONTENTS

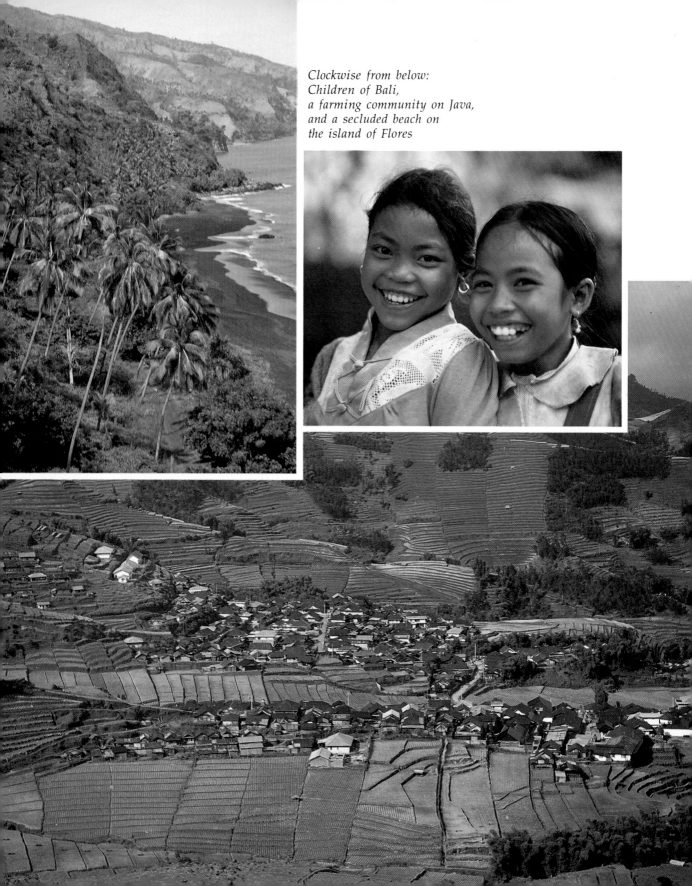

Clockwise from below:
Children of Bali,
a farming community on Java,
and a secluded beach on
the island of Flores

Chapter 1

SELAMAT DATANG,
"WELCOME!"

When visitors come to Indonesia by air, their first stop is likely to be on the tiny island of Biak, off the coast of West New Guinea. At whatever hour of day or night the plane lands, several young people dressed in native costume are there to greet the travelers. These performers play instruments, chant, and dance for a delighted audience. Behind them, windows reveal a picture-postcard, tropical scene—swaying palm trees, white sands, and a deep blue ocean. This friendly welcome introduces strangers to a unique and beautiful land.

Indonesia is a vast country, spread over thousands of islands. If you were to visit one Indonesian island every day, it would take you about forty-eight years to go to all of them. Its people represent hundreds of tribes, languages, and physical types. Nearly every kind of landscape can be found somewhere on these islands—tropical rain forests, jungle, wetlands, desert, snow-capped mountains, fertile valleys, volcanoes, and secluded beaches.

If it is judged by Western standards, Indonesia is a poor country. Yet starvation and homelessness are uncommon and beggars are almost never seen. Family and village ties are strong. It is taken for granted that relatives and neighbors care for one another and share what they have.

It is impossible to know everything about this endlessly varied nation. But certain important factors draw all Indonesians together despite their differences.

First and above all is the national motto: *Bhinneka Tunggal Ika*, which means "Unity Through Diversity." The motto means that diversity is considered an asset, not a liability.

A second unifying force is the national ideology of *Pancasila*, a five-point statement of philosophy that teaches respect for differences. The five principles are, in brief: belief in one Supreme God, just and civilized humanity, national unity, democracy by consensus, and social justice for all.

Third, a national language, Bahasa Indonesia, is spoken throughout the country, in addition to local languages and dialects. All schoolchildren learn this language and the national motto, and they study the principles of Pancasila.

These three unifying ideas underlie the government of Indonesia. In addition, the people of the islands share a long history of interaction and cooperation and, for the most part, a common religion. The great majority of Indonesians are Muslims; however, freedom of religion is guaranteed as a part of Pancasila.

Diversity has made Indonesia what it is today. As a major crossroads of ancient trade routes, it has been visited by people from far-off lands for thousands of years. These international visitors—most noticeably Indians, Malaysians, and Arabs—have left their marks.

The Garuda,
the national symbol
of Indonesia

The Hindu influence from India can be seen in much Indonesian architecture, especially on Java and Bali. India also gave the nation its national symbol, *Garuda*, the fierce man-eagle who appears on the state crest. In Hindu mythology, Garuda was the means of transportation for the god Vishnu.

Bahasa Indonesia is primarily derived from the Malay language, but some words have been added by Arab, Dutch, Indian, and English visitors to the islands. And the Islamic religion was contributed by the Arabs and Persians.

We cannot visit every one of Indonesia's islands in these pages, but we can at least begin to understand what the country is all about and why diversity has been, is now, and will continue to be such an important part of its identity.

Chapter 2

TANAH AIR KITA,
"OUR LAND AND WATER"

Brilliantly colored birds sing from the tops of trees, and monkeys swing through the vines of thickly overgrown rain forests and jungles. Snow-capped mountain peaks tower above stands of trees that perfume the air with camphor and sandalwood. Palm trees heavy with coconuts wave over wide, white beaches on hundreds of tiny, uninhabited tropical islands.

These are a few of the many different scenes that make up the fascinating country of Indonesia.

Indonesia has four times as much water as land within its borders. It is the world's largest *archipelago*, a word meaning "an expanse of water with many scattered islands."

This watery nation does indeed have many islands and islets. While many sources state that Indonesia has 13,682 islands, the latest topographical survey performed by the armed forces reported in 1992 that there are more than 17,500. Two of them—New Guinea and Borneo—are the second and third largest islands in the world. (Greenland is the largest. Australia is considered a continent, not an island.) Sections of these two large islands are part of Indonesia—Irian Jaya on West New Guinea and Kalimantan on Borneo. Many of the other Indonesian islands are very tiny and more than half have no inhabitants.

Opposite page: A rice paddy among palms and mountains on Sulawesi

Medan, on the island of Sumatra, is one of the five cities with over one million people.

The archipelago stretches farther from east to west than the distance from New York City to Los Angeles, and its distance from north to south is about the same as from New York to Miami. The island group forms a wide crescent, shaped roughly like a new moon lying on its back. It curves down and back across the equator in the waters between southeastern Asia and Australia. It is bounded by the South China Sea on the north, the Indian Ocean on the south and west, and the Pacific Ocean on the north and east.

THE ISLANDS AND SEAS

The five largest islands are New Guinea, Borneo, Sumatra, Java, and Sulawesi. New Guinea is divided between the nation of Papua New Guinea and the Indonesian province of Irian Jaya. More than two-thirds of Borneo, called Kalimantan, is part of Indonesia. The rest of the island belongs to Malaysia and the small Sultanate of Brunei Darussalam. Papua New Guinea and Malaysia are the only

The white marble Istiqlal Mosque in Jakarta

nations that have a common land border with Indonesia. Other near neighbors are Singapore, east of Sumatra; the Philippines, north of Sulawesi; and Australia, to the southeast.

Sumatra is the westernmost island. It borders on the Indian Ocean to the west. On the east the Strait of Malacca separates Sumatra from the peninsula of Malaysia. Across a narrow channel at the southeastern tip of Sumatra is the island of Java. Bali, a small but densely populated island, lies to the east of Java; and Kalimantan, on Borneo, is north, across the Java Sea from both Bali and Java.

The group of small islands east of Bali is called Nusa Tenggara (which means southeast islands) or the Lesser Sunda Islands. East of them are the Timor Sea and the Arafura Sea, then the island of New Guinea, with Irian Jaya.

East of Borneo are the Celebes (or Sulawesi) Sea and the island of Sulawesi (previously called Celebes). North of the Celebes Sea is the Sulu Sea. To the east are Maluku (known throughout history as the Spice Islands) and the Maluka (or Molucca) Sea.

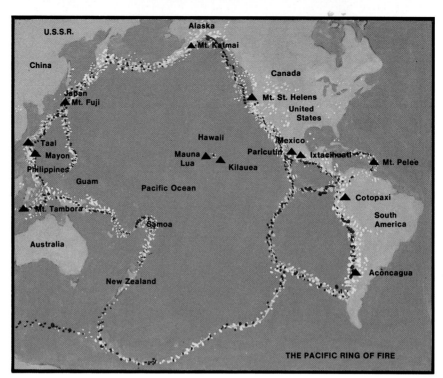

The Pacific Rim of Fire includes Indonesia. Mt. Tambora, on the island of Sumbawa, is shown just above Australia.

HOW THE ISLANDS WERE FORMED

The islands of Indonesia are among the newer pieces of real estate on the globe. Geologists tell us they were formed only about fifteen million years ago, as a result of shifts of land under the ocean and volcanic eruptions.

These occurrences, both volcanic and tectonic (which refers to movements in the earth's crustal plates), continue into the present time. Here in Indonesia, two great tectonic plates are moving very slowly toward each other: Australia is creeping northward and a huge plate under the Pacific Ocean is shifting south and west. Indonesia lies between the two plates. However, a potential collision of the two plates is thought to be millions of years in the future.

Indonesia also lies within the Ring of Fire, the nickname geologists have given to the Pacific Rim. Volcanoes are distributed

Fertile soil surrounds Agung Volcano on the island of Bali.

along nearly all the lands that border the Pacific Ocean on both sides, in the lands of Asia and the Americas alike.

Hundreds of volcanoes have helped to form and to alter the shape of the islands. Most of the country is mountainous. The highest peak is Puncak Jaya in Irian Jaya, with an elevation of 16,500 feet (5,029 meters). Streams of lava from the volcanoes have burst forth and tumbled down the mountainsides. The heat from an eruption leaves tons of ashes and debris behind. Rains eventually wash this rubble down toward the sea, often creating new lowlands near the shore.

Volcanic eruptions can be beneficial. Chemically, lava is either acid or nonacid. If it is nonacid, it helps create good, fertile soil. Volcanic craters also can serve as reservoirs to capture rainwater. Among the few places on earth where nonacid outpourings from volcanic eruptions have frequently been helpful are Java and Bali. The combination of rich soil and an excellent balance of sunshine and rain has made them two of the most fertile tropical islands in the world.

*A drawing
of the eruption
of Krakatau
in 1883*

Volcanoes also can be horribly destructive. About a hundred volcanoes in Indonesia are still active, more than in any other region in the world. Eruptions occur nearly every year. Great disasters have been caused by volcanic eruptions in recent centuries. Krakatau was a small volcanic island in the Sunda Strait, about halfway between Java and Sumatra. In 1883 an eruption of Mount Krakatau (sometimes spelled Krakatoa) with a force greater than that of several hydrogen bombs caused a tidal wave that submerged the coast of the island of Java, killing thirty-six thousand people. Earlier, in 1815, Mount Tambora on the island of Sumbawa, east of Bali, erupted in an even greater blast. The eruption and the famine and disease that followed it killed more than ninety thousand people.

GEOGRAPHIC REGIONS

Indonesia's land and water are divided into three regions, which can be described as two shelves of land under the ocean

16

with a very deep drop-off between. In the west and east, the waters are generally no more than 700 feet (213 meters) deep. In the center the ocean floor drops to depths as much as 15,000 feet (4,572 meters).

Sumatra, Java, Borneo, and several smaller islands sit on the Sunda shelf in the western part of the country. The eastern area is on the Sahul shelf, which extends north from Australia. New Guinea and some smaller islands are in this region. In between, in the deep waters, are Sulawesi and many small islands.

All of Indonesia is in what is called the "equatorial ever-wet zone." There is a heavy rainy season, from November to March, but several inches of rain fall nearly every month on most of the islands. The southeastern islands, however, usually have a long dry season between May and October, and may even experience an occasional drought. This is caused by hot, dry air air blowing up from Australia.

If all the islands were flat, temperatures would be similar throughout the country, but they are not. Differences in altitude and in rainfall cause significant variation in climate. At sea level, temperatures range from 78 to 90 degrees Fahrenheit (25.5 to 32 degrees Celsius) throughout the year. In upland towns the range is from 72 to 77 degrees Fahrenheit (22.2 to 25 degrees Celsius), and the highest mountains are cold enough to keep a snow cover year-round. Humidity is high throughout most of the islands, usually averaging from 75 to 85 percent.

PLANT LIFE

About 10 percent of all plant species in the world can be found in Indonesia.

A rain forest along the Niru River in Sumatra (above);
coffee and clove trees on Java (right)

Nearly three-quarters of the land is covered with tropical rain
forests. Tall trees form thick canopies overhead. Palms and other
shorter trees grow in their shade. Ferns, bamboo, vines, mosses,
rattan, and other plants form a tangled jungle below the trees. The
rain forests include a number of valuable trees—spice trees, such
as clove and nutmeg; fruit trees; aromatic camphor and
sandalwood; and fine hardwoods, such as teak and ebony.

Environmentalists, both in Indonesia and the rest of the world,
are concerned about the rate at which the rain forests of Indonesia
are disappearing. Ten percent of the world's total rain forest land
is found here, in an expanse greater than in any other country
except Brazil. Indonesia is the world's largest exporter of wood,
and neither local nor foreign timber companies replant enough
new trees to replace those cut. Some forests also are cleared for
agriculture, mining, and relocation of people.

Orchids (left) and the rafflesia (right), the world's largest flower

Exotic flowers abound in the rain forests; more than twenty-five hundred species of wild orchids are found in Irian Jaya. The world's largest flower, the rafflesia, grows in south central Sumatra. Its huge blooms, with five petals of reddish and white color, can grow to as much as thirty-nine inches (one meter) in diameter and twenty pounds (nine kilograms) in weight.

Forests of chestnut and oak trees grow at higher altitudes, and alpine meadows can be found on some mountain peaks. Mangrove forests flourish in tidal areas of Sumatra, Kalimantan, and southern Irian Jaya.

Patches of dry grassland and savanna appear in the Lesser Sunda Islands. They are affected by the hot winds of the dry season.

The Komodo dragon (above) is a giant lizard, while the bandicoot (left) weighs only about two pounds (less than a kilogram).

ANIMAL LIFE

A wonderful menagerie of exotic animals live in Indonesia's forests and waters. Many of them are native to Asia and Australia. A few are found nowhere else in the world. One of the rarest is the Komodo dragon, a giant monitor lizard found only on Komodo, a small island east of Bali. This creature is the world's largest lizard. An adult can grow to a length of ten feet (three meters). Other unusual animals are the bandicoot, a marsupial, and the Sulawesian anoa, a dwarf buffalo.

Tigers, rhinos, lions, elephants, wild pigs, tapirs, orangutans, and leopards are among the five hundred types of mammals that inhabit the forests. Some fifteen hundred species of birds include parrots, mynahs, cockatoos, cassowaries, and more than forty

A double-wattled cassowary (left),
a giant sea turtle (above top),
and a Borneo hornbill (above)

types of birds of paradise. Crocodiles, giant sea turtles, dolphins, and great numbers of fish and coral inhabit the seas.

The Indonesian government is very interested in preserving the nation's incredible store of wildlife. More than three hundred nature reserves, protected forests, and national parks have been set aside.

THE SURROUNDING WATERS

A great variety of marine life abounds in the oceanic waters of the Indonesian archipelago. In addition to a plentiful supply of edible fish and crustaceans, there are many species of beautiful ornamental tropical fish. These are an important export, in demand for aquariums in Japan, the United States, and Europe.

Colorful underwater life includes tube corals (left) and clown fish that live among the tentacles of the sea anemone (right)

Colorful and rare shells are collected on some of the more remote beaches of the eastern islands. However, collecting shells or other marine objects is prohibited within nature reserves.

Spectacular gardens of coral grow in Indonesia's warm tropical waters. These living organisms are found in many colors and formations. They grow into huge reefs that provide both homes and nourishment for other forms of marine life—fish, shellfish, sponges, crayfish, and underwater plants. In the Celebes Sea off the coast of north Sulawesi, the reef has formed a huge wall that drops to depths ranging from 98 to 262 feet (30 to 80 meters) before reaching the sea shelf.

Chapter 3

THE MANY FACES OF INDONESIA

Indonesia is the fourth-largest nation in the world in population, after China, India, and the United States. The 1990 census counted almost 200,000,000 people.

These millions are unevenly distributed over Indonesia's thousands of islands, more than half of which have no inhabitants at all. Four out of five Indonesians live on Java and Sumatra.

Population density—the number of persons per square mile of land—is greatest in Java and Bali. The nation has five cities with more than a million people each: Jakarta, Surabaya, Semarang, Bandung, and Medan. Only two metropolitan areas in the United States, New York and Los Angeles, are larger than Jakarta.

The people of Indonesia vary greatly in physical type and skin color. The majority are believed to be of Malay stock, descended from people who migrated from the mainland of Asia three or four thousands years ago. Some—especially the tribes in the eastern islands—resemble the Aborigines of Australia and Melanesia (islands in the Pacific Ocean northeast of Australia), with very dark skin and kinky hair. Others, also dark skinned, are

A dancer from Sulawesi (left),
young boys from the island of
Flores (above top), and a young
Sumatran girl with her sister (above)

small of stature like the pygmies of Africa. Still others are of the type called Mongolian, some with light skin and almond-shaped eyes and some with brown skin and curly hair.

Anyone who believes that the people of this earth can be neatly classified as belonging to black, brown, red, yellow, or white "races" would be astounded at the enormous diversity in Indonesia. Attempts at classification into "ethnic groups" have identified more than a hundred different cultures, whose people speak more than three hundred separate languages and dialects. Some of these languages are closely related, while others bear little or no resemblance to one another. The numbers of dialects are greatest in the eastern islands, and these dialects are less like one another than are those in the western islands.

The largest ethnic minority group is the Chinese. Because of their involvement in business and their relative wealth, the ethnic Chinese have been the target of political resentment and even riots in modern times.

The official language is Bahasa Indonesia. This language is understood and spoken by most of the people in addition to their own local dialects. Bahasa Indonesia is highly phonetic and simple to learn, because it has no articles, genders, or cases.

COASTAL AND INLAND PEOPLE

The geography of the islands is responsible for the great number of different tribes and languages. People who lived in the coastal cities were influenced by many cultures. Traders from other lands have visited the islands for more than two thousand years. Early coastal people also built their own ships and sailed abroad.

A father and son in Irian Jaya (above) and an aerial view of a small village in the jungle (right)

Life in the interior was quite different. Ancestors of inland tribes who came to Indonesia from other lands moved away from the coasts into high mountain areas. These mountains were barriers that kept people apart. Most mountain tribes lived a very isolated existence until quite recently. Modern means of transportation have opened up many doors, but there are still some tribes who have a very simple life-style and have had almost no contact with outsiders.

Dozens of different tribes live in the interior of Kalimantan on the island of Borneo. All are called Dayaks by outsiders, though they do not use this term themselves. They are probably descended from Mongolian immigrants who came to this region around 5000 B.C.

More than a million people live in Irian Jaya, the Indonesian half of the large island of New Guinea. The ancestors of these people are believed to have migrated from Melanesia. Some tribes still rely on hunting and gathering to obtain food, and their trading involves such objects as shells, bird feathers, animal skins, and arrowheads. More than a hundred different languages are spoken by scores of tribes who have little interaction with one another. Thick jungles, rugged mountains, and deep swamps, plus an almost total lack of roads, keep people close to their own villages.

RELIGION AND CUSTOM

One of the five important principles written into the official Indonesian state philosophy is "Belief in the One and Only God." Religious freedom is an important part of Indonesian political belief. The constitution protects the rights of every individual to worship according to his or her conscience. In addition, the government gives financial aid for construction of houses of worship to all religious faiths, in proportion to the number of their members.

Nearly 90 percent of all Indonesians are followers of Islam. In fact, there are more Muslims in Indonesia than in any other nation of the world. This surprises many people who think most Muslims live in the Middle East. Muslims are dispersed throughout the islands. Hindus and Buddhists are concentrated on the island of Bali.

The ancient Indonesians were animists. They believed that spirits lived in all of nature—in trees, animals, the wind, and all natural forces. Therefore, all animate and inanimate objects should be treated with respect and honor. In addition, they believed the souls of deceased ancestors continued to exist and deserved ongoing attention.

Muslims worship in a mosque (above). Most Muslim women, like these students (right), wear a head covering as a mark of their faith.

ISLAM

Each day at sunrise and sunset a Muslim "announcer," called a *muezzin*, broadcasts a chant over loudspeakers in nearly every Indonesian city and village. This is the call to prayer for devout followers of Islam.

The Muslim religion is a philosophy, a way of life, and a code of conduct; it influences the way its followers think and behave. The word *Islam* comes from Arabic and means "total submission to the authority and power of Allah (God)."

In Indonesia, Islam is not as strict and confining as in many Muslim countries. Women of Indonesia enjoy much greater freedom, for example. While many of them choose to wear a head covering as a mark of their faith, most do not veil and cloak themselves completely in the fashion found in some Middle Eastern nations.

A Christian church in Sumatra

Indonesian Muslims observe Ramadan, a month-long fast, during the ninth month of the Javanese calendar. It is not a total fast; the family eats a hearty breakfast before sunrise, nothing during daylight hours, and then they may eat again after sunset. Special prayers are said, both at home and in mosques.

Every Muslim who can possibly afford to do so is supposed to make a *hajj*, a pilgrimage or journey, to the holy city of Mecca, in Saudi Arabia at least once in his or her lifetime. The Indonesian government actively encourages and supports these activities by furnishing a number of services to the pilgrims before, during, and after their sojourns.

CHRISTIANITY

Christianity was introduced to the islands in the sixteenth century by Portuguese and Spanish traders who converted quite a

*A Hindu priest (above) and a decorated
sculpture at a Hindu temple (right)*

few of the people of Maluku to the Roman Catholic faith.

Later the Dutch colonists, most of whom were Protestants, built churches that some of the Indonesians joined.

Today about one of every ten or eleven Indonesians is Christian. Most of them are concentrated in Maluku, North Sulawesi, and North Sumatra.

HINDUISM

Hinduism was introduced into Java by travelers from India in ancient times. The Hindu religion is polytheistic; it recognizes many gods and goddesses. However, many Hindus believe that all their traditional gods and goddesses are just different forms of one supreme being; thus they can reconcile their religious beliefs with the acceptance of one god as mandated by Pancasila.

When the early Javanese princes accepted Hinduism, they did not give up all of their early animistic beliefs—they simply

The tiny temples in a Balinese family compound (above) and a dance mask used in Hindu temple festivals (right)

combined the new ideas with them. This process is called syncretism. As later Indonesians converted to Islam, Christianity, and other religions, they too syncretized the new creeds with their traditional beliefs.

Several centuries ago a great many Hindus left Java for Bali rather than convert to Islam. Hinduism has survived in Bali ever since, and today 95 percent of the Balinese are Hindus. Massive, ornate stone sculptures of Hindu gods are everywhere. Daily offerings are laid at their feet and they are draped with flowers for holidays. Every family compound and major office complex has tiny temples where prayers are offered.

Balinese Hinduism has strong elements of Buddhism, animism, and ancestor worship, and it permeates all aspects of everyday life. It includes a belief in reincarnation and that how one spends this life will determine the level of future existence. Over the centuries a religion unique to Bali has evolved, but it has deep roots in Hindu traditions.

Chapter 4

FROM JAVA MAN TO
HINDU KINGDOMS

There is no single early history of this vast group of islands called Indonesia. For countless thousands of years, many different groups lived in isolated inland areas, with little contact with outsiders. They formed tribes and villages, learned how to raise food and how to make goods necessary for survival, but we know very little about them. There are no written records and, with some exceptions, very little archaeological evidence to tell us about those ancient times.

Along the seacoasts, however, the story is different. Long before written history began, coastal people built boats and ships, sailed to other lands, and traded goods with strangers who came to their shores. Their history is easier to trace.

THE JAVA MAN

In 1890 on the island of Java, a Dutch scientist named Eugene Dubois made a discovery that stirred up the entire scientific world. He found some fossils that resembled the bones of modern humans.

Dubois believed he had found evidence that an ancestor of the human race lived in that part of the world hundreds of thousands of years ago. When his findings were published, arguments began between scientists who believed in evolution and "creationists," people whose religion taught that the world was created by God, from nothing, not by evolving. Dubois was so upset with the widespread criticism of his discovery that he gave up the study of primitive people.

Archaeologists have since found other specimens in this region and elsewhere that confirm the authenticity of Dubois's discovery. The so-called Java Man was a primitive form of human who lived about half a million years ago.

THE STONE AND BRONZE AGES

The period before people began to use metal is called the Stone Age. In parts of Indonesia it lasted until about 1000 B.C. Stone Age people used stone tools, and the earliest tribes hunted and gathered their food. They were nomads who made temporary homes in caves.

Even before the Stone Age ended, there were waves of immigration to the islands. People came from India, China, and other parts of Asia and intermarried with the native men and women. From about 500 B.C. to A.D. 500, immigrants from China had great influence over the life of people in the islands. They brought a Bronze Age culture with them, the use of metal to make tools, utensils, and ornaments. The island people began to grow rice in irrigated fields, to make pottery, and to fashion clothing out of bark cloth. They began to use the arts of music and puppetry for entertainment and ritual. They built boats and ships

Rice fields planted on terraces, or graduated steps

to sail between the islands, and even traveled as far away as India.

To maintain irrigation systems for growing rice, it was necessary to organize a sort of village government. Groups of villages were then united by strong leaders into small feudal kingdoms.

Traders from India were sailing into ports on Java, Sumatra, and south Celebes (now called south Sulawesi) for several hundred years before the birth of Christ. Sumatra's east coast borders the Strait of Malacca, the gateway to the South China Sea and trade with China. The sea-lanes traveled by merchant vessels from China and India brought traffic to the islands. By 200 B.C. the port cities were engaged in a flourishing commercial trade.

An ancient Javanese myth tells that once upon a time only spirits lived on the island. Then so many people came to live there that the spirits were crowded out and forced to live in the volcanic craters or in the sea. Thus the Javanese believed that their world began with migration. The story illustrates how blurred the line is between ancient legends or myths and fact.

A sequel to this story is still portrayed in Java's shadow-puppet shows. It tells of Semar, a man who acts as a clown, who promised that only evil spirits would be driven out. He declared himself to be a *dayang*, or guardian spirit, who would protect Java's kings and princes.

JAVA AND SUMATRA

More is known about the early history of Java and Sumatra than is known about most of the other islands. Some of the knowledge comes from archaeological findings and some from ancient Indian and Chinese writings. For example, Chinese documents dating from the second century A.D. mention the existence of diplomatic relations between China and Java.

As more Indians visited the islands, they began to have an influence on the thinking and life-style of Java's local rulers. The highest caste of Indian society was the Hindu priests, called brahmans. These social and cultural leaders were sophisticated and well educated. The Javanese and Sumatran kings were eager to learn from them.

Traces of early Indian influence can be seen today throughout the region. The religions—Hinduism and Buddhism—were brought into the islands from India. Most of the kings adopted one or the other of these religions and embraced a great deal of Indian philosophical thought.

The brahmans taught the local leaders about navigation, astronomy, architecture, and the healing arts. They helped devise

A worker in a batik factory

improved systems of government, legal practices, and military organization. They contributed certain Sanskrit words to the local native dialects. Indian methods of wet-rice culture and animal husbandry spread through the countryside.

Ptolemy, a noted geographer, astronomer, and writer who lived in Alexandria, Egypt, during the second century A.D., described Java in his writings. He wrote that it was a country with a good system of government and that knowledge of agriculture, navigation, and astronomy was well advanced. He also mentioned that the Javanese used a base-ten number system and metal coins and that they were adept in metalwork and the art of *batik*, a method of textile printing.

In Indonesian history, the entire period from ancient times until the sixteenth century (when Europeans began to seize power in Indonesia), is called the Period of Hindu Kingdoms.

KINGDOM OF SRIVIJAYA

Hindu and Buddhist traders controlled much of the sea trade for several centuries. Hindu and Buddhist city-states sprang up along the east coast of Sumatra. One of the most important was the kingdom called Srivijaya, located near the site of the present-day city of Palembang.

Srivijaya was a renowned educational center and a cosmopolitan community. Its location gave it a great deal of control over the trade that passed through the Strait of Malacca. By the second half of the seventh century, Srivijaya had become the first major Indonesian sea power. Local boat builders manufactured the largest ships in the world at the time.

Trade involved merchants from Persia (present-day Iran), Arabia, and India. Frankincense and myrrh from the Middle East were exchanged for silk, porcelain, and medicinal products from China, as well as spices and precious woods from the islands. Pearls, coral, precious stones, camphor oil, ivory, tin, iron, and woolen and cotton cloth were among the goods carried through the strait.

The Arab traders also brought the religion of Islam to Indonesia and established Islamic trading centers along Sumatra's coast. Marco Polo, a Venetian traveler who was one of the first writers to tell the world about the Far East, visited Srivijaya on his way home from China in 1292. He observed the presence of Muslims in the region.

Srivijaya held control over the strait for several centuries, until a successful attack by the Javanese kingdom of Majapahit in 1377 changed the balance of power.

The Borobudur Temple (above) has one large stupa, shrine, *and many small* dagobs, *miniature stupas, on the top. Most contain a statue of Buddha. The large stupa is missing its spire. A close-up of the back of some of the dagobs (right)*

JAVANESE KINGDOMS

A great Buddhist kingdom called Sailendra flourished in central Java from about A.D. 750 to 850. Arts and culture reached a high level, and the kingdom was a commercial and naval power. Borobudur, the largest Buddhist temple in the world, was built during this period. The temple, near the city of Yogyakarta, has been extensively restored. Today, twelve centuries after its construction, it is visited by tourists from all over the world.

Ruins of many other temples in Java, both Buddhist and Hindu, attest to the advanced knowledge held by early Javanese of architecture, engineering, and construction methods. They also are evidence that the two religions existed side by side without conflict.

The Prambanan temple (above) is being restored. The remains of a monument from the Singasari kingdom (above left)

Toward the end of Sailendra's power, a Hindu kingdom called Mataram was emerging in central Java. The major architectural achievement of this kingdom was the temple complex named Prambanan, also near Yogyakarta. This national treasure is being restored.

These ancient temples are more than great accomplishments to be admired; they also are a "textbook" for students of Indonesian history. Hundreds of bas-relief panels carry illustrations of religious legends, history, and the life of the period.

King Dharmawangsa headed a powerful kingdom called Singasari in east Java toward the end of the tenth century. He codified laws and ordered the translation of Indian literature into Javanese.

The power of the Srivijayan Empire based in Sumatra was

beginning to decline, and a distinctive Javanese culture was emerging and spreading its influence into Bali.

The last important Hindu power in Java was the Majapahit Kingdom, founded in 1293. First Srivijaya, then the rest of Sumatra, was conquered by the Majapahits.

Kublai Khan, a thirteenth-century Mongol emperor of China who had conquered Burma, Cambodia, and other parts of southeast Asia, tried to expand into the Indonesian region. His forces invaded Java, but they were repelled.

The next century is sometimes called early Indonesia's Golden Age. The Majapahits controlled most of the coastal regions of Sumatra, Borneo, Sulawesi, Maluku, Sumbawa, and Lombok. They can be credited with establishing the first great Indonesian commercial shipping empire. Diplomatic relations and firm economic ties with China, Vietnam, Cambodia, Annam, and Siam (Thailand) added to the strength of the kingdom.

A hundred years after its founding, the Majapahit Empire began to crumble. Many local leaders converted to Islam and set up independent Muslim states.

BALI

The small island of Bali, just east of Java, is much better known to the rest of the world than many of Indonesia's larger islands. It is an important center of native arts and crafts, and nearly all of its people are still Hindu, not Muslim as is most of Indonesia. The Balinese language is derived from a dialect of southern India.

The earliest written records of civilization in Bali date from the ninth century. By this time the arts of metalwork, stone sculpture, and wood carving were already well developed.

The island was divided into princedoms. Rice culture, requiring a complicated irrigation system, was a primary source of food.

During the eleventh century the histories of Bali and Java began to merge. A wise and strong leader, King Airlangga, rose to power in Java. His mother, after the loss of her husband, married a Balinese prince, and the two courts were linked. Airlangga built waterworks along the Brantas River that are still being used today. He encouraged the arts; novels written during this period are still being studied in universities in several countries of Southeast Asia. After his death, descendants of his mother ruled a semi-independent Bali for two centuries.

Over the years a succession of Javanese kings tried to take control of Bali, but local princes resisted them. In 1343, Javanese armies of the Majapahit dynasty invaded the island. A Javanese brahman was appointed king of Bali, and many of the Javanese nobles moved to the Balinese capital.

SULAWESI

The island of Sulawesi, formerly called Celebes, has a most unusual shape. It consists of four long, narrow, irregular peninsulas joined in the center. The interior is mountainous and covered with an almost impenetrable thick jungle, where isolated tribes have lived for centuries. In contrast, some of the coastal cities were early ports of call on the busy trade routes.

More than half the people on the island live in the southwestern peninsula. There are three major tribes, or groups—the Bugis, Makassarese, and Torajans.

Legends say the Torajans came to the island from somewhere in Indochina by boat and sailed upriver to the mountains of the

SULAWESI

MALUKU

BALI

The traditional ship-shaped houses of Tanatoraja

interior. When they arrived they used their boats to form the roofs of their houses. This architecture is very picturesque and is still used for many new homes and other buildings in Tanatoraja (Torajaland).

The Bugis and Makassarese are coastal, seafaring people. Although their languages differ, they have much in common. Nevertheless, there is a history of rivalry between the two groups, as well as between the Bugis and Torajans.

The northern peninsula, a long arm pointing east and northeast toward the Philippines, also has a long history of sea trade and contact with other countries. Here, as on other islands, the territory was divided into a number of small kingdoms.

MALUKU

Maluku, often called the Spice Islands and the Moluccas, was a group of islands well known to the ancient world. The Roman

A variety of vegetables and spices for sale at the market

historian Pliny, who lived in the first century A.D. , described the trade in spices between these islands, Africa, and Rome.

For centuries before modern refrigeration and other methods of preserving food were invented, spices were highly prized by people in the Western world. The spices covered up the taste of the not-too-fresh food. They were also rare and expensive, since they had to be imported from far-off lands. For these reasons, plus the fact that they took up very little space on shipboard in relation to their value, they became extremely important to maritime trade and to the merchants who traveled to Europe on caravan routes.

Once Indian, Chinese, and Arab traders discovered that cloves, nutmeg, and mace grew only in Maluku (or the Moluccas), these islands became among the most visited in the Indonesian archipelago.

The Hindu kingdoms had only a minimal effect on life in the rest of the islands that make up modern Indonesia. The trade routes included occasional stopovers on Borneo, New Guinea, and the

Marco Polo wrote about the Far East.

group of small islands east of Bali known as Nusa Tenggara (southeast islands), but most of the people on these islands lived inland and had little or no contact with the outside world before the European period.

THE RISE OF ISLAM

Traders from Persia and Arabia had been coming to the Indonesian islands for many centuries. In the mid-thirteenth century some of the Hindu kings began to convert to the Islamic religion. When Marco Polo visited northern Sumatra in 1292, he reported that the port of Perlak was a Muslim city.

There were three types of kingdoms on the islands at that time. Coastal kingdoms were urban, and the economy depended on the maritime trade. Rural inland kingdoms were agricultural. Their strength came from their surpluses of food and the manpower to produce it. Then there were the tiny Maluku kingdoms. They were agricultural, but they produced spices almost exclusively. They raised very little food.

It is easy to see how the three different types of communities needed one another. The kingdoms that did not produce their own food imported from those that did. All of them depended on the ports for the textiles, porcelains, medicines, and precious metals and gems imported from foreign lands and for the wealth brought to the region by the export of spices.

The Islamic traders lived in the coastal cities, sometimes for months at a time, waiting for favorable sailing weather. Traders were important to the economy, especially of the coastal cities, and they were strong allies of native rulers who converted to Islam.

The dominant Islamic sect in the region was Sufism, a mystical brotherhood that used dance, poetry, and trances in their worship. The animist-Hindu rulers found this new religion quite compatible with their own culture.

The once-powerful Majapahit kingdom in Java declined as the Muslim influence emerged. A number of the local princes converted. But toward the end of the fifteenth century a great many nobles, scholars, and cultural leaders fled to Bali rather than give up Hinduism.

Bali already had a rich culture of its own. Music, dance, painting, various crafts, and learning were all highly developed and appreciated. The addition of so many of Java's most creative artists and scholars to this environment fueled a unique tradition that has continued to modern times.

At first the conversion of Javanese rulers was peaceful, but in 1527 troops of the *sultan* (the title given to Muslim rulers) of Demak attacked and conquered the capital of the west Java kingdom, the site of present-day Jakarta. The conquerors drove the rulers out, confiscated agricultural lands, and took control of much of Java.

By this time, however, people from Europe had taken an interest in the islands. Forces were set in motion that led to a long period of European domination.

Chapter 5

COLONIAL PERIOD

Jayabaya of Kediri, a twelfth-century ruler of a Javanese kingdom, wrote a book in which he prophesied that at some time in the future Indonesia would be ruled by a white race. Following their long rule, these people would be driven out by members of a yellow race who would come down from somewhere in the north but would not rule for long. After that, according to this early seer, Indonesia would gain permanent independence from foreign occupation.

Modern students of history have seen Jayabaya's predictions come true. Europeans did, in fact, control the archipelago for more than three hundred years. Most of that time the white foreigners were Dutch. Then, during World War II, a yellow race arrived from the north; armed forces from the empire of Japan invaded the islands. Under Japanese occupation, all Europeans were rounded up and sent to concentration camps. After World War II Indonesia gained its modern independence.

FIRST CAME THE PORTUGUESE

In the winter of 1497-1498, a Portuguese explorer named Vasco da Gama made a voyage that forever changed the balance of trade

Around the time of Vasco da Gama (left), camels were used to transport goods overland (right).

around the world. A fleet of ships under his command was the first to sail from Europe to Asia around the Cape of Good Hope on the southern tip of Africa. Before the discovery of this new route, Europeans had been dependent on traders in the Middle East who brought goods from Asia partway by sea, then by long overland caravan treks. Now ships under the flags of Portugal, Spain, Holland or the Netherlands, and other countries of Europe could manage their own Far Eastern trading.

Da Gama sailed to India, and a few years later four Portuguese vessels found their way to the port of Malacca on the Malay Peninsula. The sultan of Malacca, not wanting to anger the Muslim merchants, drove the Portuguese off. But another Portuguese fleet, with more men and ships, came back a couple of years later and captured Malacca.

The Portuguese established a chain of forty trading posts in the region and achieved a dominant position over trade in the Spice Islands for much of the sixteenth century.

While the Portuguese did not establish a lasting position of power in the Indonesian archipelago, they left a few cultural legacies. Some of them married native women and had children. They contributed a number of Portuguese words to native languages. They converted about twenty thousand Indonesians to Catholicism. A few of the former Portuguese communities still have a large percentage of Christians, though many of them changed to Protestantism during the period of Dutch colonization.

THE DUTCH EAST INDIES

The first arrival of Dutch ships in Indonesia was a fiasco. The first four ships landed in Banten, the leading port of the pepper trade, in 1596. The Dutch crew, tired and sick after a long voyage, behaved so badly on shore that the local prince drove them back to their ships and refused to trade with them. Captain Cornelis de Houtman kept the sailors aboard while he visited several ports along Java's coast in search of spices. But when they got to Bali the whole crew deserted, and it took the captain a long time to find enough sailors to make the voyage home.

Even though de Houtman acquired only a small amount of spices to take back to Holland, the prices they brought in Europe were so high the expedition was a modest success, financially. Speculators soon found out about it. Five Dutch investment groups were put together the very next year to send more ships to the Indies.

Holland was the commercial center of northern Europe at the turn of the seventeenth century. Recognizing great opportunities for profits in trade with the Indies, a large group of Dutch traders got together in 1602 and formed the Dutch East India Company,

The Dutch built Batavia (pictured above in the seventeenth century), which was modeled after cities in Holland.

or VOC (the initials of the name in the Dutch language). In 1602 the government of the Netherlands granted a charter giving the VOC the power to negotiate treaties, raise armies, and wage war in Asia on behalf of the Netherlands.

In those days the European nations regarded the little-known lands in Asia, Africa, Australia, and the Americas as places for exploitation. They believed that people of any color other than white were inferior and that they should be taught, controlled, and Christianized by the more "civilized" people of Europe. The only question was how to carve up this world. The Dutch set their sights on the East Indies.

At first the VOC faced stiff competition for the spice trade from English, Spanish, and Muslim merchant ships. In 1614 a forceful and ambitious Hollander named Jan Pieterszoon Coen was put in charge of the company's operations. He mapped out a military course to extend the Dutch power in the region. Coen built a series of small fortifications along the north coast of Java. Within four years he had destroyed the capital city of Jayakarta and built a new one on its site. It was copied closely after cities in Holland and given a new name, Batavia.

In spite of attempts on the part of various princes and sultans to resist the invaders, the Dutch had gained control of the entire archipelago by the end of the seventeenth century. The small kingdoms and sultanates were too weak and divided to resist the power of Dutch militarism.

Over the next hundred years, however, profits from the East Indies trade began to decline. By the end of December 1799 the two-hundred-year-old VOC, thought to be rich and invincible, was bankrupt. The government of Holland decided to take over the assets of the defunct VOC. The islands were declared a colony, known as the Dutch East Indies.

A BRIEF ENGLISH RULE

Meanwhile, in Europe things were in turmoil. France had invaded Holland in 1795. From then until the defeat of France's emperor, Napoleon, in 1815, the Dutch government was controlled by France.

During this time, in 1811, the British East India Company took temporary control of Indonesia. Sir Thomas Stamford Raffles was declared lieutenant governor-general of Java and dependencies under the supervision of the governor-general in Bengal, India.

Raffles was a wise scholar and a good governor. During his brief tenure he initiated a degree of self-government, abolished the slave trade, and did away with the Dutch system of forced agricultural labor. He initiated restoration work on some of the ancient temples and wrote a history of Java. His reforms did not last long, however, because the British gave the colonies back to Holland in 1815 after the French were defeated in Europe and the Dutch government was restored to full power.

A local court under Dutch rule

In 1825 a young Javanese prince launched a guerrilla war against the Dutch colonial government. The rebellion continued for five years, supported by some, but not all, of the Javanese aristocrats. More than 8,000 Dutch and 200,000 Indonesian lives were lost during this conflict—more from starvation and illness than from actual fighting.

A new harsh period of domination began after the Java War. The Dutch government had a huge national debt, and the leaders intended to use profits from the colonies to finance it. They forced native farmers to grow large quantities of certain crops for the government, even when there was not enough land left to support the farmers and their families. This was known as the "cultivation system." Severe famines in certain areas resulted.

Some politicians in Holland were opposed to the policy of government-controlled agriculture, and from time to time certain reforms were legislated. But in general, the native people were given only tiny wages, they were forced to pay high taxes, and they lost control of their lands and their own destiny. The system was not very different from the operation of the large slave plantations in the southeastern United States. The colonists justified their actions by claiming, as have many other slaveholders and exploiters worldwide, that the Indonesians were content and were being raised from savagery to a more enlightened existence.

However, the government never had complete domination over all of the archipelago at any one time. Native kings still controlled some areas, and many battles were fought. The sultanate of Aceh, in northwest Sumatra, was especially rebellious. Warfare raged there for more than thirty years.

In Bali and Lombok, kings and noblemen demonstrated their opposition to the colonial masters by committing *puputan*, "royal suicide." On three different occasions groups deliberately marched into Dutch gunfire.

THE RISE OF NATIONALISM

One of the effects of the long, harsh period of Dutch domination was to bring about a greater desire for unification of the islands than had ever existed before. In the early years of the twentieth century several Indonesian nationalist movements started.

Java was becoming increasingly Europeanized as the century began. Dutch colonists introduced many elements of modern civilization—gaslight, newspapers, trains, automobiles, shops, hotels, and factories. They also provided educational opportunities for some privileged Indonesians. These young people studied European philosophy and government. Many of them became active in organizations that formed the nucleus of a nationalist movement. Indonesians were not alone in these activities; stirrings of anti-imperialist sentiment were arising in colonial territories all over the world.

Budi Utomo, "noble conduct," founded on May 20, 1908, was Indonesia's first significant nationalist organization. Its members were students and intellectual leaders. It began as an educational club, but soon turned to politics. Over the next few years several other important associations were formed.

A trade association of Muslim merchants formed a political party named *Sarekat Islam*. It held a convention in 1916 and resolved to demand independence from the Dutch.

Toward the end of World War I the Dutch gave the Indonesians the so-called November promise—a promise never kept—to grant self-government to the colony. Instead, as economic conditions worsened in the 1920s the government placed severe restrictions on Indonesian civil liberties.

These measures did not stop the nationalist movements from organizing. In 1927 some of the leaders took part in the first international convention of the "League Against Imperialism and Colonial Oppression," held in Brussels. Later that year a young man named Sukarno (many Javanese have only one name) founded the Indonesian National party. Sukarno was not the only important leader of the freedom movement, but he is the one best known to the outside world because he later became the first president of independent Indonesia.

On October 28, 1928, at the second Youth Congress in Batavia (Jakarta), the following three-part pledge was adopted:

> "We, the sons and daughters of Indonesia,
> recognize one homeland, Indonesia.
> "We, the sons and daughters of Indonesia,
> recognize one nation, the Indonesian nation.
> "We, the sons and daughters of Indonesia,
> honor the language of unity, Bahasa Indonesia."

Sukarno (left) and Muhammad Hatta (right) were held in custody by the Dutch for almost ten years.

This pledge is frequently repeated even today. The Indonesians hold it in the same esteem as Americans do their Pledge of Allegiance.

The Dutch government was uneasy about these small but constant indications that Indonesians were in a rebellious mood. The leaders, including Sukarno, were arrested on more than one occasion and exiled to a remote island. Sukarno and another leader named Muhammad Hatta were held in custody from 1933 until the Japanese invasion of 1942 during World War II.

The leaders of the independence movements tried to negotiate with the Dutch for self-government, but the colonial government rejected all suggestions for change. As one governor-general declared, the Dutch had "been here for 350 years with stick and sword and will remain for another 350 years with stick and sword."

Indonesian villagers chat with a Japanese officer in 1942.

In 1940 German troops marched into the Netherlands, to begin an occupation that lasted for the duration of World War II. Still the Dutch government in Indonesia remained stubbornly in charge and even tightened some of the restrictions imposed on the Indonesians.

JAPANESE INVASION

In January 1942 everything changed. Soon after the Japanese attacked Pearl Harbor in Hawaii December 1941, they sailed into one Indonesian port after another. The Dutch army on Java was small, and the Indonesians had not been permitted to have any military forces of their own. The Japanese quickly advanced. Within a few weeks the Japanese occupied Batavia (present-day Jakarta) and soon destroyed much of the Dutch navy.

On March 7, 1942, the governor-general of the Netherlands East Indies surrendered to Japan. Very quickly, all Europeans in the region were rounded up and sent to concentration camps.

At first the Indonesians were elated at these events, viewing the Japanese more as liberators than as new masters. The old

Sukarno gives his inaugural address as Indonesia's first president.

prophecy that foretold the coming of a yellow race of rulers had said these would remain for only one harvest season. Moreover, the Japanese freed the nationalist leaders who had been imprisoned by the Dutch, gave some of the administrative jobs formerly held by the Dutch to Indonesians, and decreed that the Dutch language was banned and replaced by Bahasa Indonesia.

But the Japanese were in Indonesia for their own purposes. They needed bases there, and their war machine needed many of Indonesia's resources. They robbed the countryside of rice, rubber, and oil. They stole gold and precious stones from the cities. They forced Indonesian women into prostitution. The islanders soon recognized that Dutch colonialism had merely been replaced by Japanese imperialism.

Japan surrendered to the Allies on August 15, 1945. Two days later, on August 17, Sukarno and Hatta proclaimed Indonesian *merdeka*, "independence." The new Republic of Indonesia was born. A constitution was adopted as the basic law of the country. Sukarno became the nation's first president, Muhammad Hatta was vice-president, and the first cabinet was formed.

Chapter 6

INDEPENDENT INDONESIA

By the end of World War II, Indonesian leaders had decided their nation was now going to be independent and self-governing. On August 17, 1945, Sukarno and Hatta, two of the men who had been active in the freedom movement for many years, issued the following Declaration of Independence.

> We, the people of Indonesia, do hereby proclaim the
> independence of Indonesia. All matters pertaining to
> the transfer of power . . . will be carried out
> expediently and in the shortest possible time.

British forces landed in Indonesia shortly after the war ended, as representatives of the Allied forces. Their purpose was to disarm and round up the Japanese troops that had occupied the country. Dutch troops arrived, also, as the Dutch colonists were not inclined to give up their wealth and power in the islands easily. Fighting went on between the Dutch and the Indonesian freedom fighters for the next four years.

The new, independent government carried on negotiations with the Dutch and the British, and the Dutch grudgingly conceded

Enthusiastic crowds greet President Sukarno in front of the Presidential Palace.

control over Java, Sumatra, and Madura, an island off Java's coast—but not the rest of the Dutch East Indies.

Prime Minister Jawaharlal Nehru of India called a conference of nineteen nations, in New Delhi, to consider Indonesia's problems. The conference drew up a petition to the United Nations. In January 1949 the United Nations Security Council called on the Dutch for a cease-fire and release of the thousands of Indonesian political prisoners. At first the Dutch defied this resolution. They did not withdraw from Indonesia and even declared to the world that the Indonesian government and army no longer existed.

At the end of 1949, however, the Netherlands officially recognized the sovereign Federal Republic of Indonesia. The Dutch East Indies ceased to exist. The new government had a constitution and a parliamentary system under which the president and his Cabinet were responsible to the Parliament.

THE SUKARNO DECADES

Within a few months, President Sukarno decided that a federal government in which Parliament had power over the executive branch was too weak. He felt that a spread-out country like Indonesia needed a strong central government to unite and integrate its many different kinds of people. In August 1950 the Republic of Indonesia became a unitary state; Parliament was no longer superior to the president and his Cabinet.

On September 28, 1950, Indonesia became a member of the United Nations. The Dutch still claimed control over Irian Jaya (West New Guinea) and the Portuguese still held East Timor, but the rest of the islands were part of the republic.

Sukarno was not sure what to do about the extensive foreign holdings in his country. Over the next few years he became increasingly anti-Western and anticolonial.

In April 1955 President Sukarno hosted a conference of twenty-four Asian and African countries, known internationally as the Bandung Conference. Its purpose was to promote cooperation in economic, cultural, and political affairs among newly independent nations, and nonalignment with either side in the Cold War. The conference adopted the *Dasa Sila*, "Ten Principles," of Bandung, to promote world peace, respect for one another's sovereignty and territory, noninterference in a country's internal affairs, and recognition of the United Nations' principles of human rights.

In 1956 President Sukarno adopted a more authoritarian policy of "guided democracy." Sukarno nationalized all the Dutch holdings in Indonesia—agricultural estates, banks, factories, and commercial companies—and cut off all trade with the Netherlands in 1958. He expelled the Dutch people living in the islands.

A beaming President Sukarno

After three hundred years of Dutch colonialism, nearly all traces of the Netherlands were erased from the landscape. In many other countries formerly under colonial rule, the colonists' language, at least, remains, but Dutch is nonexistent in Indonesia today. The most widely spoken foreign language in the islands is English.

The government took further measures to discourage foreign ownership of business in Indonesia. A Petroleum Law declared that all petroleum belonged to the state and that exploration and development rights must be leased from the government. Restrictions were placed on taking any business profits out of the country. Import licenses and visas for foreign business personnel became quite difficult to obtain. Sukarno's speeches contained references to "imperialist capital," saying it would interfere with the establishment of socialism.

An atmosphere of economic uncertainty resulted from these measures; the infrastructure (roads, bridges, electricity, and so forth) was neglected. Inflation developed. Political unrest grew at times during these years. Java, then as now, had the majority of the population, but the greatest wealth came from the other

Indonesian Chinese in Java, who were thought to be Communists, had their houses and shops destroyed.

islands. People on these outer islands began to feel that the government spent too much money on Java and not enough on other areas. As a result, some rebel movements grew. Especially in 1956 and then again in 1965, *coups*, or efforts to oust those in power, were attempted.

In 1965, as a result of military action against the new nation of Malaysia and a vote against Indonesia in the United Nations General Assembly, Indonesia withdrew from membership in the United Nations. This was a further step toward Indonesia's isolation. During that same year, the Indonesian Communist party made an unsuccessful attempt to take over the government. Six army generals were assassinated. General Soeharto (sometimes spelled Suharto), commander of the army's strategic reserve, led troops who regained the national radio station that had been taken over. Soeharto ultimately was successful in thwarting the coup. But in this effort, it is estimated that more than 100,000 persons thought to be Communists were killed. Many more were arrested. The impact of this purge is still felt in Indonesia today.

By this time Indonesia was nearly bankrupt. The failure of Sukarno's economic policies was obvious. Nevertheless, he was still popular enough that his opponents were reluctant to depose him.

THE NEW ORDER GOVERNMENT

Unrest continued. Between October 1965 and March 1966 Sukarno was still president, but in name only. On March 11, 1966, Sukarno gave Soeharto supreme power to restore order. During 1966 the Communist party was officially banned. By March 1967 Sukarno was stripped of all power, and General Soeharto was named acting president. In 1966 membership in the United Nations was resumed, and the country reverted to an open-door policy for foreign investors. Certain properties that had been confiscated by Sukarno were offered to their former owners. In 1967 Soeharto formed the "new order government." The following year Soeharto was elected to a five-year term as president. He was reelected in 1973, 1978, 1983, 1988, and 1993.

Sukarno, the father of independent Indonesia, was no longer a political force. He died on June 1, 1970.

President Soeharto has made economic development a major goal of his government. He proclaimed a series of five-year plans, beginning in 1969, which helped the economy in many ways.

Priority was given at first to improving agricultural methods and increasing rice production to make the country self-sufficient for food. Early achievements were improvements in irrigation systems and transportation.

Among other natural resources, Indonesia possesses a great deal of petroleum. The worldwide boom in oil prices that started in

*President Soeharto shows his ballots before
voting for representatives in 1988.*

1973 was very helpful to the government. From 1974 to 1989, the
five-year plans focused on improving the general standard of
living—better food, clothing, housing, education, and health
services. Government expenditures for these goals paid off in
higher literacy rates and fewer Indonesians living below the
poverty level. Fewer children died in infancy and life expectancy
statistics improved dramatically.

The five-year plan of 1989 gave increased attention to industrial
development. As revenues from oil exports dropped, the
government actively worked to expand and diversify the
economy.

Even though his regime has faced many problems, President
Soeharto has been reelected again and again. During the 1970s
there were uprisings led by guerrilla bands in Kalimantan and
Irian Jaya. Islamic leaders felt the state government was
undermining their authority; riots erupted over a new marriage

law that did not follow Muslim precepts. Student groups demonstrated in protest against government corruption and inflation.

The 1980s brought new problems. Petroleum prices dropped dramatically and the country suffered a severe depression. The government devalued the Indonesian currency by 27 percent.

Progress toward true democracy and implementation of the ideals of Pancasila have been marred from time to time by loss of lives during uprisings, imprisonment for political dissenters, and press censorship.

Separatist movements have given the Indonesian government trouble in three regions: Aceh, a province in northern Sumatra; East Timor; and Irian Jaya.

Aceh is an area rich in coal and other minerals, yet the local population has not received much benefit from these riches. Acehnese people resent the domination of their area by a state government based in Java. Government-sponsored resettlement of many Javanese people into Aceh has fanned the flames of this resentment. Military force was used in 1990 to put down a rebellion. Hundreds of people were killed and some were imprisoned. Others fled to Malaysia for refuge.

In Irian Jaya there are a number of people who would prefer to be united with their neighboring country, Papua New Guinea, rather than continue as a part of Indonesia. Major conflicts occurred in 1979 and 1984, and thousands of refugees fled across the border. Discussion about border issues between the two nations led to a border agreement signed in 1990. Consulates have been established in towns on both sides of the border, and about one-third of the refugees have voluntarily returned to Irian Jaya.

East Timor was under the control of Portugal until 1975 when

Antigovernment demonstrators in East Timor

Portuguese troops withdrew. Indonesia sent in troops to prevent the small region from declaring independence, and on July 17, 1976, East Timor was proclaimed the twenty-seventh province of Indonesia. Australia and New Zealand officially recognized this annexation, but the United Nations General Assembly has passed several resolutions asking that Indonesian troops be withdrawn from the province.

Bitter fighting has broken out from time to time between the government troops and guerrilla rebels. The situation has been made even worse by widespread famine and disease and reported atrocities. Portugal and the United Nations are concerned about the problems and the Indonesian government has engaged in talks with Portugal in an effort to resolve them.

PANCASILA

One school subject all Indonesian children are required to study before they enter high school is Pancasila. This is the word for the official political philosophy of the country. It consists of five principles:

1. Belief in one Supreme God
2. Just and civilized humanity
3. The unity of Indonesia
4. Democracy guided by the wisdom arising out of deliberations among representatives of the people
5. Social justice for the whole of the people of Indonesia

These five principles were stated in the constitution drafted and adopted in 1945. Indonesia changed constitutions several times between 1945 and 1959, finally returning to the 1945 constitution on July 5, 1959. However, the Pancasila has continued to be the basis of Indonesian law and government; it cannot be changed.

Belief in One Supreme God While the vast majority of Indonesians are Muslims, the Pancasila allows for freedom of worship for all faiths based on belief in one God.

Just and Civilized Humanity Oppression of any human beings by any others, whether by other Indonesians or foreign nations, is not to be tolerated.

The Unity of Indonesia No group of any tribe, ancestry, or skin color is superior to any other. Loyalty to the nation and all of its people is essential. President Soeharto has said that the differences among Indonesians "should blend us together to perfect harmony like the beautiful spectrum of the rainbow."

Representative Democracy Pancasila democracy depends on decision-making through *musyawarah*, "deliberation, talking things through," to arrive at *mafakat,* "consensus." All political decisions should be based on the other four principles of Pancasila.

Social Justice for All the People of Indonesia All natural resources of the country should be used to further the greatest possible good and happiness of all the people. Justice means protection of those who are weaker from exploitation by those who are stronger.

These five principles are goals for Indonesia, but like many goals have not always been achieved in fact.

STATE GOVERNMENT

Indonesia's constitution of 1945 provides for an elected Parliament and limited separation of powers among the several branches of government. In practice, however, both presidents Sukarno and Soeharto have held a great deal of power over all branches.

Members of the armed forces have played important roles in the nation's history. The military is looked on as a unifying force among the diverse ethnic, religious, and political groups of the country. The nation enjoys good relations with neighboring countries, so the role of the military is more active in internal affairs than in protection from outside aggression.

State government in Indonesia refers to the national administration. There are six branches of state government: People's Consultative Assembly, Presidency, House of Representatives, Supreme Advisory Council, State Audit Board, and Supreme Court.

The Republic of Indonesia is divided into twenty-seven provinces, three of which are called special territories.

A meeting of village administrators in Bali

LOCAL GOVERNMENTS

The government of the twenty-seven provinces in Indonesia follows the pattern of the state, with an executive branch headed by a governor and a provincial legislature. The legislature elects two or three candidates for the office of governor. The president appoints one of these candidates upon the recommendation of the minister of home affairs.

Below the provincial level are district and village administrative units.

FOREIGN RELATIONS

In general, Indonesia enjoys good relations with other nations of the world. Consistent with the policy of nonalignment, diplomatic relations are maintained with China, Russia, and the United States, as well as with the neighboring countries of Southeast Asia.

Because of the problems in East Timor and Indonesia's policy of press censorship, relations between Indonesia and some other United

President Soeharto (third from left) poses with members of ASEAN and other countries who met in 1990.

Nation member nations have at times been strained.

In 1967 Indonesia joined with Thailand, the Philippines, Malaysia, and Singapore to found the Association of Southeast Asian Nations (ASEAN). In 1984 Brunei became a sixth member of ASEAN. Through this organization, the nations cooperate in promoting regional economic, social, and cultural advancement. Among other activities, they work together to increase tourism to that part of the world. Indonesia, as a member of ASEAN, played a role in seeking a solution to problems between Cambodia and Vietnam.

As a member of the Non-aligned Movement (NAM), Indonesia also tried to negotiate a settlement of the Iraq-Kuwait crisis of 1990. Indonesia condemned the invasion of Kuwait, but refused to take part in the multinational military effort against Iraq.

In September 1992 Indonesia hosted the tenth NAM Summit Conference in Jakarta and assumed the chairmanship of the organization for a three-year term. NAM was founded by 29 developing nations in 1961 and has since grown to a membership of 108 nations plus 20 groups or nations classified as observers. The Jakarta summit was attended by 100 member nations and 19 observer nations.

Chapter 7

MAKING A LIVING

More than half the citizens of Indonesia live off the land. Rice is the most important food crop in the western islands, where the majority of the people live. Sago, a starchy fruit that grows on palm trees, and tubers such as yams and taro are common in the eastern and southeastern islands.

A small percentage of Indonesia's agricultural people practice the "slash-and-burn" method of agriculture. The Indonesian word for this is *ladang*. A ladang farmer clears a forest plot by burning the trees and cutting away the underbrush. If the burning is done just before the rainy season, the ash and debris help to fertilize the soil. This method raises concerns because of the loss and destruction of forest lands.

More than 90 percent of the nation's farmers live in densely populated areas, where they need methods that produce much more food per acre than ladang farming can achieve. Fortunately, most of these areas also have fertile soil and abundant water. Here the farmers have practiced wet-rice cultivation for generations. They have cleared and terraced the land, leveled and diked the

Opposite page: Rice is the most important food crop in the western islands.

Fresh vegetables for sale in a bustling market

terraces, and devised elaborate irrigation systems. This is *sawah* farming, and while it requires a lot of hard work, it is normally very productive. The combination of tropical climate and fertile land results in several crops each year.

Farmers also raise vegetables and animals—sheep, hogs, buffalo, and chickens—for sale in local marketplaces. In some areas, village cooperatives and government agents help provide credit and marketing services, as well as agricultural instruction, fertilizers, and seed to improve farm production.

ESTATE FARMING

Ever since early traders discovered the valuable harvest of the Spice Islands, crops for export have been among Indonesia's main assets. Large plantations were established during the Dutch colonial period to produce export items. Some of these large

People gather to help unload the catch from fishing boats (above).
These pickers are almost lost to view in the lush growth of
a tea plantation in Java (right).

holdings still exist. Rubber and sugar are the most important
commercial export crops. Sizable quantities of tobacco, palm oil,
coffee, tea, cocoa, and cinchona (a tree bark used in medicine) are
also produced.

FISHING

Fishing is a way of life for many people who live along the
coastlines of the Indonesian islands. Some families make their
homes on boats. Fish is the main source of protein in Indonesia.
Fish are caught in the oceans and rivers and are stocked in lakes,
ponds, and flooded rice paddies as well. Commercial fishing is
done primarily in small areas of inshore waters, especially in
northern Java.

An oil rig on Sumatra

NATURAL RESOURCES

Indonesia is one of the world's leading suppliers of oil, primarily in the form of crude oil and natural gas. Indonesia is also the world's second-largest producer of tin. All domestically produced tin ore is smelted (refined) locally before being exported. There are large deposits of bauxite, the ore from which aluminum is made, on Sumatra. Most of the bauxite mined on the islands is exported to Japan.

There are coal deposits on Sumatra and Kalimantan, nickel on Sulawesi and in the Maluku group, and copper on Irian Jaya. Indonesia also has large quantities of iron that have not been mined yet, as well as smaller deposits of many other minerals.

Another major source of Indonesia's income is timber. Teak and other valuable tropical hardwoods are in much demand by foreign buyers. The most accessible forests are on the islands of Kalimantan and Sumatra.

Unloading timber from sailing schooners

The government is making an effort to protect large forest regions and to replant some of the areas that have been overcut. Soil erosion, floods, water shortage, and damage to irrigation systems are among the negative results of overcutting, especially on Java. Even though timber is one of Indonesia's most important exports, bans have been placed on the export of raw logs in favor of creating wood-using industries, such as the manufacture of furniture, within the country.

INDUSTRY

Indonesia is rich in natural resources, but its leaders realize that foreign investment is needed to develop a modern industrial society. At the same time, they are understandably nervous about allowing foreign interests to own businesses within the country, because of Indonesia's long history of colonial exploitation.

Foreign investment has been important to the Indonesian

*Raw latex drips
into a pot from a
cut in a rubber tree.*

economy since the beginning of this century. The Dutch owned
and kept the profits from the plantations and some of the oil
wells. The United Kingdom had investments in oil, rubber, and
manufacturing. Belgium, Denmark, Switzerland, the United States,
France, and Norway all held rubber estates on northern Sumatra.

In 1958 the government of Indonesia seized all the Dutch assets
and enterprises on the islands. That same year a foreign
investment law was passed that made certain guarantees to some
of the other businesses owned by foreigners. This law was
nullified in 1965 by Sukarno, who nationalized several oil
companies and rubber plantations. He then ordered the seizure of
all remaining foreign property in the country.

After Soeharto became the head of government, Sukarno's
policy was reversed. President Soeharto encouraged foreign
investment, but tried to safeguard Indonesian interests by setting
certain restrictions on foreign-owned businesses. These called for
a certain percentage of each enterprise to be owned by
Indonesians and required the companies to train Indonesians to
take part in management.

A fertilizer plant

In the spring of 1992 the Indonesian government decided to make investment even more attractive to foreign businesses by allowing selected new businesses to start up with 100 percent foreign ownership. The new measure does require foreign investors to transfer ownership to Indonesian interests gradually. Incentives are given for investment in the less developed regions of the country. Industries that are labor-intensive—that is, those that create a great many jobs for Indonesian citizens—are especially welcome.

The government's attitude toward foreign investment is constantly changing, but the goals are to balance economic growth with protection of both the people and the natural resources of the nation.

Goods currently being manufactured in Indonesia include machinery and machine tools, automobiles, aircraft, textiles, and chemicals. Processed materials for export include plywood, palm and coconut oils, cement, fertilizers, steel, and processed foods.

Chapter 8

EVERYDAY LIFE

Javanese fishermen, professional men and women in Sumatra, Balinese craftspeople, rice farmers in Kalimantan, and deep-sea diving instructors in north Sulawesi all live very different lives, yet they have much in common. Even though millions of Indonesians have flocked to the crowded cities in search of employment, most of them have roots in an ancestral village.

Major village decisions are made by the elders, who try to deliberate until they come to a harmonious agreement. Cooperation is the goal. Courtesy is very important, as is *adat*, "custom, or common law." Families live, work, and play together—not just father, mother, and children but grandparents, aunts, uncles, and cousins, too.

EDUCATION

Schooling through the primary grades in Indonesia is compulsory and free. According to the constitution, all education

Opposite page: A Balinese father and his children on a motorbike

Primary students (left) and a class in a
rehabilitation center for the handicapped (right)

must be nondiscriminatory. The supply of teachers and schools is
beginning to catch up with the need—almost 100 percent of the
nation's children aged seven to twelve are now enrolled in school.

Through the third grade, teaching may be done in a regional
dialect, but after that everyone is taught in Bahasa Indonesia.

Some schools are run by the government and some by religious
and other private groups. Private schools receive government
subsidies if they meet required standards. Most of them are
coeducational. Students normally wear uniforms, such as identical
batik shirts or blouses with skirts or trousers of a prescribed color.

The school system consists of six primary grades, three years in
middle school, and three years in high school. There are fifty-one
universities and a number of specialized vocational schools in
Indonesia.

High school students

THE ROLE OF WOMEN

Raden Kartini was Indonesia's first women's emancipationist. She was born in 1879, the daughter of a noble family, and died at the age of twenty-four while giving birth. During her short life she wrote a series of letters to friends criticizing the restrictions placed on her as a female by the Javanese *adat* system. These letters have been widely published and read, and a holiday in her memory is celebrated each year on April 21.

Women's organizations were active in Indonesia's struggle for independence. The first Indonesia Women's Congress, representing fifty women's organizations, was held in Yogyakarta in 1928, and Bahasa Indonesia was used for the first time as an official language at that meeting. During the fighting with the Dutch after August 1945, women were active in the battlefields, doing intelligence and courier work, preparing food for the guerrilla fighters, and giving first aid.

Women serve in the army auxiliary corps.

According to the constitution, discrimination against women in rights, duties, jobs, pay for equal work, and politics is forbidden. However, these ideals are far from total achievement.

An associate minister for the role of women has the responsibility for working toward the goal of equality through several programs. They include extending the level of education of women, which is especially low in many rural areas; providing information and assitance in the areas of health, nutrition, sanitation, and family planning; training in skills that can help raise family income; and working toward changes in the attitudes of both men and women regarding equality.

Marriage laws have been liberalized considerably, and a number of other laws have been passed to assist women in achieving their constitutional rights. Nevertheless, the percentage of women in middle and upper positions in the work force and in political office remains very low.

University students

On the plus side, there is no obvious discrimination in education from the primary through the university, and women enrolled in higher education study a wide spectrum of disciplines.

FOOD

Rice is the staple in the diet of the western Indonesian islands. All traditional foods are designed to be an accompaniment to rice. In other regions people may depend on sago or yams as their staple food. Fish is the major source of protein.

Sumatrans use a variety of fiery hot spices in their cooking. Javanese dishes are milder, delicately seasoned, and sometimes a bit sweet.

In fertile rural regions families live on what they grow for themselves—rice, vegetables, fruit. When the *sawah*, "rice fields," are flooded, the farmers raise fish and eels in the waters. Surplus

Above: Sate *are small pieces of meat on a skewer grilled over charcoal and served with peanut sauce, and* ayam *means chicken.   Below: Rice for sale in the market (left) and a vendor preparing a* martabak, *or pancake (right)*

A succulent buffet of Indonesian cuisine

crops are taken to the market for sale, and sometimes the need for cash is so great that the families keep very little for themselves.

Two favorite dishes are *nasi goreng*, "fried rice," and *mie goreng*, "noodles," mixed with bits of vegetables and delicately seasoned. Indian curries and Chinese dishes are popular.

Warung, fast-food stalls, are found in cities and villages. They serve *martabak*, a kind of pancake; *sate*, skewered meat in peanut sauce; *bakmi* or *yoakmi*, noodles; fish and shellfish; and frogs' legs.

A fancy Indonesian meal served in certain restaurants all over the world is *rijsttafel*, a Dutch word meaning "rice table." This feast consists of rice accompanied by a large selection of Javanese and Sumatran dishes. Side dishes might include grilled king crab, spicy beef with grated coconut, spiced eggs, baked bananas wrapped in dough, dried beef with potato chips, sweet and sour fish, mackerel in red chili sauce, mixed vegetables, jackfruit and chicken in coconut milk, shrimp sate, egg bean curd, fried grated coconut with peanuts, fried chilies with shrimp paste, crackers, and pickles. Indonesians have a soup to start and a dessert afterward.

Volleyball is a popular sport.

SPORTS AND RECREATION

Indonesians enjoy many kinds of sports. They are among the best badminton players in the world. Soccer is very popular, as are tennis and volleyball.

On the island of Madura, bulls are bred to be used in racing competitions. West Sumatrans use ducks for the same purpose. Children compete in kite flying in West Sumatra.

In some parts of the country young people like to go biking. There are many areas for superb snorkeling and scuba diving.

Families (in the cities) watch television and videos for entertainment, or go to zoos or parks. Outside Jakarta is a large theme park called *Taman Mini Indonesia Indah*, ''Indonesia in Miniature.'' It contains a collection of houses and pavilions from all over the country, displays of regional handicrafts and clothing, plus many restaurants, museums, theaters, an orchid garden, and a bird park. On Sunday afternoons this park draws so many people it is almost impossible for anyone to move about.

A general view of Taman Mini Indonesia Indah, *"Indonesia in Miniature"*

Chapter 9

INDONESIAN ARTS AND CRAFTS

It has been said that every Balinese person is an artist, even if he or she has a job driving a bus or working in a resort hotel. After working hours, everyone is involved in some way in the arts.

But Indonesia's artists and craftspeople are not found on Bali alone. They are all over the islands, involved in weaving and decorating textiles; making puppets and performing puppet shows; dancing traditional dances; playing in *gamelan*, or percussion, orchestras; or carving, painting, sculpting, and designing a wide variety of craft items sold at the many marketplaces throughout the islands.

TEXTILES

Textiles play more than a practical role in this culture. Used for making clothing, Indonesian textiles are also a show-and-tell of the many histories and heritages of the people. Some of the textile

Opposite page: Bamboo instruments are sometimes used to accompany dancers.

*Left: Weaving yarn into fabric
Above: A worker prepares batik
cloth for a second dye bath.*

traditions are said to date back at least two thousand years. In the
Banggai islands off the east coast of Sulawesi, there is even a
community of traditional weavers called the *Alune* tribe, a word
meaning "the people who weave."

The art of textile designing has a basis in tradition and
symbolism. Spinning, dyeing, and weaving the yarns into
materials has been regarded as a symbol of creation, particularly
birth itself. This creation was almost exclusively performed by
women in the community. The dyeing procedure was done in
total privacy. Those involved in the dyeing were not allowed even
to talk about death, and pregnant or sick women were forbidden
to participate in this part of textile manufacture.

Batik is the most familiar form of textile production in
Indonesia. It is primarily done in Java, but it can be found in other
areas as well. The cloth is painted with a *canting*, a penlike
instrument that dispenses wax over the material. The wax resists

The batik is taken from the dye bath (left) and then the wax is scraped off the fabric (right).

dyes. (The word *batik* is derived from a Javanese word meaning "fine point.") Using the wax, designs are sketched on the fabric, usually white cotton or silk. Then the fabric is dipped in dye. After the first dip, the wax is scraped off, more is applied to create more patterns, and the fabric is dipped again. The waxing and rewaxing are done for as many dips and colors as are needed in the final design.

Indonesians use batik for much of their clothing—shirts, *kebaya*, (blouses), and sarongs—oblong pieces of cloth tied around the hips or over the chest and worn by men and women alike. Some of the less expensive batiks are done by mass-production called *batik cap*. The wax patterns are stamped instead of drawn on the fabric. This procedure takes less time, which increases productivity and lowers the price.

Recently, textile workers in Jakarta have been working with a process of silk screening that looks almost identical to authentic

After dyeing, a worker removes the dye-resistant fibers (above). Then the ikat *is stretched on a frame so it can be woven (left).*

batik. Although this system meets the demands of mass marketing, it may also threaten the artistic perseverance and hard work of the craftspeople, who cannot possibly compete with such output. However, handcrafted batik is not yet obsolete, and the beauty that has kept the art alive for hundreds of years may very likely keep it thriving for hundreds more.

Ikat is a method of decorating and designing cloth in the weaving process, somewhat like tie-dyeing. The dyeing is done before weaving. Some threads are tied with dye-resistant fibers to prevent the dyes from penetrating. Sometimes gold or silver threads are used in the borders.

In addition to cotton, silk, and other standard threads, some Indonesian weavers use bark cloth, grasses, leaves, and bamboo to make textiles. Bark cloth, found in some of the more isolated areas of Sulawesi, Flores, Timor, and others, is made by weaving together strips of tree bark beaten thin, then painting the cloth. *Koffo*, "Manilla hemp," cloths are made by braiding natural fibers such as leaves, palm fronds, and bamboo. Geometric patterns are dyed into the material, which is often used to make clothing on Sulawesi, Sangir, and Talaud.

On many Indonesian islands, certain handmade textiles are traditionally used as payment for a bride. On Buton, small squares of cloth were used as money for many centuries. "Ship cloths," once found in areas of Sumatra and so named because the fabric's patterns often showed a ship loaded with people and animals, were at one time essential adornments at all-important events like births, marriages, and deaths. Some textiles are used to decorate homes. Handcrafted textiles often contain designs and symbols with religious associations, and all of them are evidence of unique artistry and craftsmanship.

WAYANG

Wayang, a Javanese word meaning "shadow," refers to one of the most popular and delightful forms of Indonesian theatrical performance—puppet shows. Shadow puppet shows are performed on Java for special occasions such as weddings, birthdays, and reunions—often just for entertainment. Shadow puppetry is a fascinating form of storytelling. It is a display of long-trained talent and artistry, plus a portrayal of life's lessons— particularly the struggle between good and evil.

The person behind the puppets (or below them, actually, since wayang puppets are manipulated by sticks connected to their arms, legs, heads, and torsos and manipulated from beneath), is called a *dalang*. A dalang (traditionally a man, but there are also a number of women dalangs) has studied this performing art for eight years or so, and has practiced daily to master the form and carry the show.

Above: The gamelan orchestra accompanies the puppet show.
Left: An artist paints a leather puppet that will be used in a shadow play.

The skill used to be one that was passed down from father to son, but now there are dalang schools on Java where puppeteers are trained. Puppeteers must learn two or three languages used in performances; the legends the shows are based on; and the gestures, movements, and voices of each of the more than three hundred puppet characters. They must learn to conduct and combine the music of the gamelan orchestra with the execution of each passage, each scene, each skit of the entire performance.

The dalang's job is not an easy one. A traditional wayang lasts hours, very often starting in the evening and playing on until the early morning hours. The dalang works all of the puppets himself, using both hands. Sometimes he even uses his feet to pound a rhythmic percussion. He creates all the voices and tells all the stories, using the folklore and adding some lively improvisation. He must act, sing, and move constantly, sometimes bringing as many as one hundred puppets to life in one night.

He performs from behind a screen, seated low on the ground out of sight from the spectators in front. However, it is not uncommon for an audience to gather behind the set to watch the master's exciting performance.

There are a number of different types of wayang. Wayang kulit is performed entirely in shadow. *Kulit,* "leather," puppets are fashioned out of leather made from young water buffalo hide. The two-dimensional puppets (they look a little like paper dolls), cut in fine detail and sometimes painted, are moved about in front of a light to cast moving shadows onto the screen between the dalang and the audience. The *halus* (good guys) figures are small and almost elegant. They stand with their legs close together with heads bowed slightly, and their gestures are smooth and tidy. The *kasar* (bad guys) are bigger, with burly, rounded bodies. They

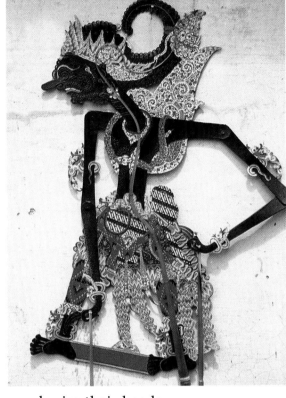

Above: Presenting a shadow puppet show
Right: Close-up of a completed leather puppet

move clumsily, speak in booming voices, and raise their heads defiantly. But wayang puppets are not all good or all bad. Each one has some good and some bad traits, and each has to struggle inwardly over both forces. Thus Indonesian art reflects life, portraying complex individuals who are not one-sided.

All the puppets are ugly, deformed, gross caricatures of humans, even the halus. It was not always like this. Wayang puppets were originally designed in the images of people, but according to Islamic teachings, it is sacrilegious to create anything resembling men and women. So, with the coming of Islam, the Javanese redesigned their puppets into exaggerated creatures that were no longer a clear representation of the human form.

Wayang *golek* uses three-dimensional, wooden puppets similar to marionettes. Like the kulit, they are manipulated by sticks rather than strings. The wayang golek is not a shadow puppet show; a screen is not used. These performances are usually

Wayang golek *figures*

presented during daytime, while the wayang kulit is traditionally an evening event.

Wayang *topeng* and wayang *orang* shows are performed by dancers mimicking the movements of puppets. They depict the same legends and moral stories as the puppet shows. In the topeng all roles are played by men who wear masks like golek puppet heads. Sometimes they speak their own lines, but more often the dalang speaks for them.

Wayang orang dancers do not ordinarily wear masks, unless they are portraying monkeys, birds, or monsters. Their costumes are like those of golek puppets. The actors often say their own lines, although the dalang takes part, also.

The most popular legends used are taken from two ancient Hindu epics. The *Ramayana* is an account of the adventures of prince Rama who conquered evil forces (a king named Ravana) who had kidnapped Rama's wife Sita. The *Mahabharata* tells tales of great warfare.

A warrior dance, performed at temple ceremonies

Wayang has begun to expand beyond traditional ceremonial presentation to modern mass-media uses. Wayang puppets are often seen today on Indonesian television, making public service announcements.

DANCE

Dance performances in Indonesia are actually dramas. They tell stories, usually with a purpose. Historically, Indonesian dance is ritualistic, done by priests, princesses, or *shamans* (healers) — or even whole tribes — to accomplish something. A dance may be one of exorcism, choreographed to drive away evil; of courage, to prepare for battle; or a celebration of victory.

Barong *dance of Bali*

Styles and purposes of the dances differ from one island culture to another. The Balinese perform trance dances. These are accompanied by heavily rhythmic sounds—the pounding of drums, clanking of chimes, or a steady chant in monotone without any instrumentation. The hypnotic rhythms and the jerking, repetitive movements of legs, arms, heads, and bodies heighten a feeling of a trance state.

The Balinese *barong* dance involves a whole troupe of dancers who portray warriors, a witch, and a benevolent beast called the barong. There is a struggle between good and evil and, of course, good is victorious.

Another Balinese dance, the *kechak,* is based on the Ramayana.

The kechak *dance*

Prince Rama is on a quest to rescue his wife, Sita, who has been kidnapped by an evil king. In his quest, along with many others, Rama joins forces with Sugriwa, king of the monkeys. Dancers portray the king's army of monkeys. They sway back and forth, raising their hands and waving their fingers in unison, making precise and identical monkeylike movements. No instrumental music is used to provide background for the dance. Instead, the

A master teacher instructs a young girl in the movements of the legong *dance (left).*
A performance of the legong *(right)*

performers chant repetitive syllables resembling the chattering of monkeys—''kechak-achak-achak-achak''—to create a vocalized and syncopated percussion sound.

The Balinese *legong* is a graceful dance performed by young girls in bindingly tight, golden costumes. The movements are quick and smooth and made to look easy.

Court dances, originally choreographed and performed for royalty, are popular in central Java. As might be expected, these are elegant, glittering spectacles. The dancers have spent years in training, conditioning their bodies and muscles to do such amazing things as bending their hands backward until the fingers touch the forearms, or simply not moving at all, holding one intricate pose for many, many minutes. The gestures are slow, deliberate, trancelike, elongated to the point of exaggeration.

Some of the smaller instruments in a gamelan orchestra

GAMELAN MUSIC

Gamelan music has often been described as the sound of "liquid moonlight." A gamelan orchestra consists primarily of percussion instruments, instruments that produce sound when they are beaten or struck, rather than being blown or strummed. The Javanese word *gamel* means "hammer," and many of the gamelan instruments are played with a type of gamel.

There can be as few as five different instruments in a gamelan orchestra or as many as fifty. Brass gongs of various sizes are hung from ropes or laid flat in wooden frames. There are "keyed" instruments like xylophones, with each key sounding a different note, and instruments with strings to be plucked. Sticks are used to play bronze kettles of many sizes and drums with goatskin or cowhide heads. Bamboo, brass, animal hides, wood, and strings are materials used to make instruments not familiar to most Western musicians.

Some of the large gamelan instruments

The gambang *section of the gamelan orchestra*

The names of gamelan instruments ring like the sounds they make. A *kenong* is a small gong. *Kendang* are drums made from hollowed tree trunks. The hard wooden bars of the *gambang* are struck with sticks made of buffalo horn. A *celempung* is a stringed instrument that is plucked, a *suling* is a bamboo flute, and a *rebab* is a two-stringed instrument played with a loosely tied horsehair bow.

Singing is a part of gamelan performances, too, but this tradition started only in the nineteenth century, while the instrumental ensembles have been around for hundreds of years. Indonesian musicians say that gamelan music symbolizes a tree: the low notes are the roots, solid and strong; the trunk is the melody; and the tinkling and rolling of the lighter, higher instruments represent branches, leaves, and flowers.

Gamelan is a special part of Javanese and Balinese cultures. The orchestras play at celebrations, festivals, and concerts. Outdoor concerts are given by very large groups of musicians playing the

Indonesian craftspeople: a silversmith (left) and a basket weaver (right)

largest and loudest of the instruments. Gamelan music is essential to the puppet shows of the wayang, important to many Indonesian dancers, and a staple of every Indonesian festivity.

In Bali, village music clubs often own gamelan instruments. The clubs perform at special events in the village and represent the village at events elsewhere. The members of the clubs maintain the instruments and work together in a spirit of *gotong royong*, or "mutual help."

ARTS AND HANDICRAFTS

The Indonesian government is very supportive of the handiwork of its native artists, realizing that such support helps a culture to survive and prosper. In recognition of the value of the country's ancient art treasures, the government pays a reward for any ancient artifact found and turned in. This appreciation also encourages today's artists to continue creating.

Balinese wood carvers (left) and stone sculptors (right)

The arts and crafts of Bali are known worldwide, yet surprisingly, there is no Balinese word for "art" or "artists." There always have been carvers or painters who created certain objects, and while these people were respected for their skill, their talents were not considered anything extraordinary. They did what they had to do; it was their function in the community to provide whatever creative service was needed. Today, however, Bali is filled with artists. They cater to tourists eager to buy hundreds of objects that range from mass-produced statues of ancient gods to priceless carvings and paintings.

Artistic expression in Indonesia is as big as a house and as small as a shadow. It's as loud as a big orchestra and as soft as a

handsome reed flute. It's in all things and places. From basket making to designing a unique building, from playing a drum to dancing the *serimpi*, every region of Indonesia has its own voice and handiwork. The serimpi is a traditional Javanese court dance originally performed only by princesses. When Javanese dance schools were established in the twentieth century, serimpi became the standard dance taught to all young women.

There is unity through diversity. Indonesian art is like the islands themselves, spread wide and covering lots of ground, existing through countless centuries. It represents an ancient heritage, yet it is also a dynamic and vital part of this nation's march to the future.

Map from Worldmaster Atlas
© 1993 by Rand McNally, R.L. 93-S-39

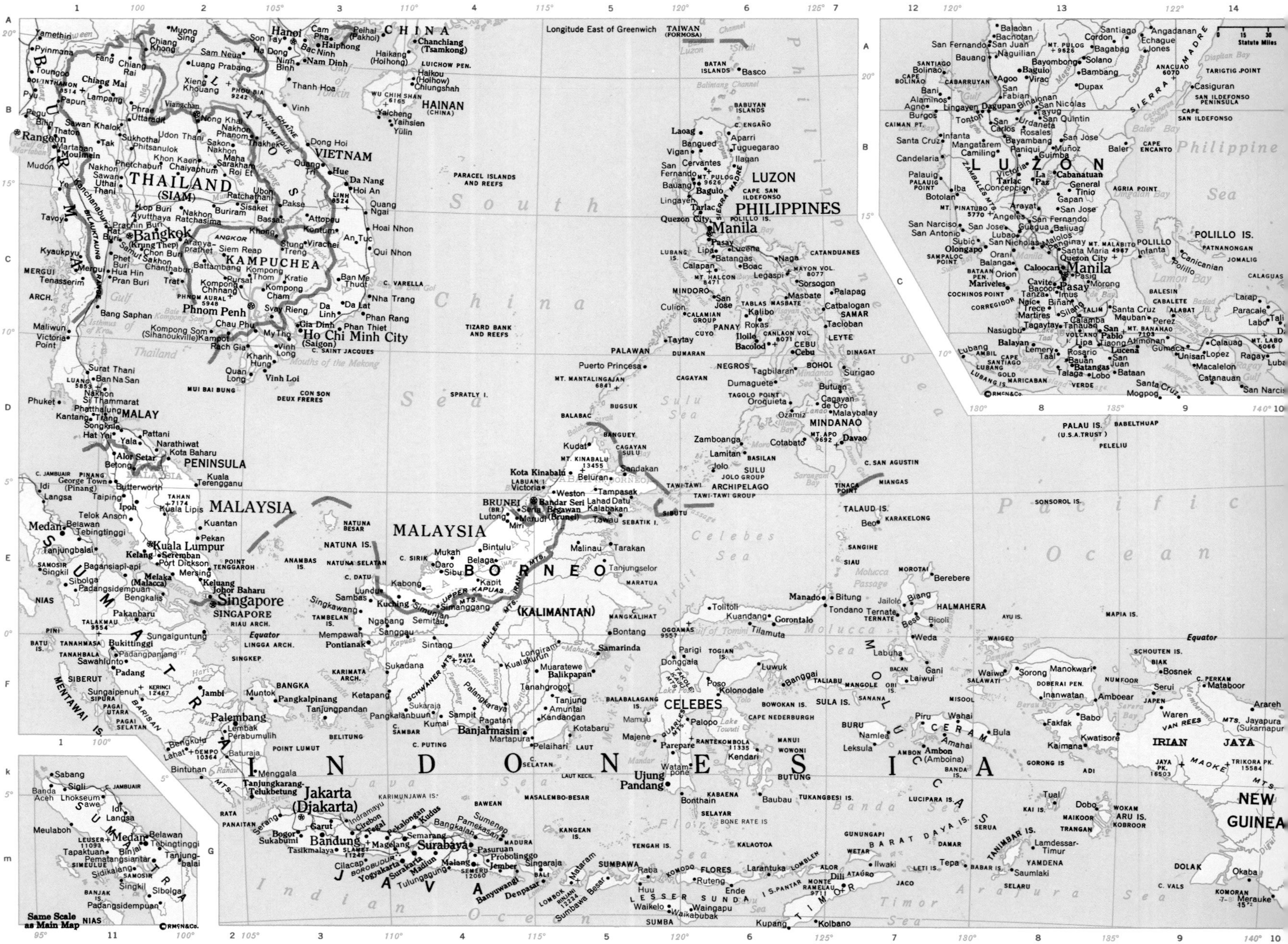

CHINA

HAINAN (CHINA)

VIETNAM

THAILAND (SIAM)

KAMPUCHEA

BURMA

LUZON

PHILIPPINES

Manila

MALAYSIA

MALAY PENINSULA

Singapore

BORNEO (KALIMANTAN)

BRUNEI

SUMATRA

JAVA

Jakarta (Djakarta)

INDONESIA

CELEBES

MINDANAO

NEW GUINEA

IRIAN JAYA

TAIWAN (FORMOSA)

South China Sea

Philippine Sea

Pacific Ocean

Indian Ocean

Celebes Sea

Sulu Sea

Banda Sea

Timor Sea

Arafura Sea

Java Sea

Gulf of Thailand

Hanoi

Bangkok

Phnom Penh

Ho Chi Minh City

Rangoon

Kuala Lumpur

Same Scale as Main Map

MAP KEY

Adi (island) F8
Alor (island) G6, G7
Amahai F7
Amboear F8
Ambon (Amboina) F7
Ambon (island) F7
Amuntal F5
Anambas Islands E3
Arafura Sea G7, G8, G9
Arareh F9
Aru Islands G8
Atauro (island) G7
Ayu Islands E8
Babar Islands G7, G8
Babo F7
Bacan (island) F7
Bagansiapi-api E2
Balabalagang Islands F5
Bali (island) G4, G5
Balikpapan F5
Banda Aceh k11
Banda Islands F7
Banda Sea F6, F7, G6, G7
Bandung G3
Bangai F6
Bangka (island) F3
Bangkalan G4
Banjak Islands m11
Banyuwangi G4
Barat Daya Islands G7, G8
Barisan Mountains F2, G2
Barito (river) F4
Batu Islands E1, F1
Baturaja F2
Baubau G6
Bawean (island) G4
Belawan E1, m11
Belitung (island) F3
Bengkalis E2
Bengkulu F2
Benjarmasin F4
Beo E7
Berau Bay F8
Berebere E7
Besa E7
Biak (island) F9
Biang E7
Bicoli m11
Binjai E1, m11
Bintuhan F2
Bitung E7
Bone Rate Islands G6
Bontang E5
Bonthain G5
Borneo (island) D5, E3, E4, E5, F4, F5
Borobudur (ruins) G4
Bosnek F9
Bowokan Islands F6
Bukittinggi F2
Bula F8

Buru (island) F7
Butung (island) F6, G6
Cape Datu E3
Cape Jambuair D1, k11
Cape Mangkalihat F5
Cape Nederburgh F6
Cape Perkam F9
Cape Puting F4
Cape Sambar F4
Cape Selatan F4, F5
Cape Vals G9
Celebes (island) E5, E6, E7, F5, F6, G5, G6
Celebes Sea D6, E5, E6
Ceram (island) F7, F8
Cilacap G3
Cirebon G3
Damar (island) G7
Dampier Strait F8
Dempo (mountain) F2
Denpasar G5
Digul (river) G9, G10
Dili G7
Doberai Peninsula F8
Dobo G8
Dolak (island) G9
Dongala F5
Ende G6
Fakfak F8
Flores (island) G5, G6
Flores Sea G5, G6
Gani F7
Garut G3
Gorong Islands F8, G8
Gorontalo E6
Gulf of Bone F6, G6
Gulf of Mandar F5
Gulf of Tolo F6
Gulf of Tomini E6, F6
Gunungapi (island) G7
Halmabera (island) E7, F7
Hari (river) F2
Huu G5
Idi E1, m11
Ilwaki G7
Inanwatan F8
Indian Ocean E7, G2, G3, G4, G5, H3, H4, H5
Indragiri (river) F2
Indramayu G3
Iran Mountains E4, E5
Irian Jaya F8, F9
Jaco (island) G7
Jailolo E7
Jakarta (Djakarta) G3
Jambi F2
Japen (island) F9
Java (island) G3, G4
Java Sea F3, F4, F5, G3, G4, G5
Jaya Peak (mountain) F9
Jayapura (Sukarnapura) F10
Jember G4
Kabaena (island) G6

Kahayan (river) F4
Kai Islands G8
Kaimana F8
Kalaotoa (islands) G6
Kalimantan E3, E4, E5, F3, F4, F5
Kampur (river) F9
Kandangan F5
Kangean Islands G5
Kapuas (river) E4, F3, F4
Karakelong (island) E7
Karimata Archipelago (islands) F3
Karimata Strait F3
Karimunjawa Islands G4
Kayan (river) E4, E5
Kendari F6
Kerinci (mountain) F2
Ketapang F3, F4
Kobroor (island) G8
Kolbano G6
Kolonodale F6
Komodo (island) G5
Komoran (island) G9
Kotabaru F5
Kualakurun F4
Kuandang E6
Kudus G4
Kumai F4
Kupang H6
Kwatisore F8
Labuha F7
Lahat F2
Laiwui F7
Lake Poso F6
Lake Ranau F2
Lake Towuti F6
Lamdessar-Timur G8
Langsa E1, m11
Larantuka G6
Laut (island) F5
Laut Kecil (islands) F5
Leksula F7
Lembak G5
Lembek E1, m11
Lesser Sunda Islands G4, G5, G6, G7, H5, H6
Leti Islands G7
Leuser (mountain) m11
Lhokseumawe k11
Lingga Archipelago (islands) F2
Lombok Strait G4, G5
Lomblen (island) G6
Lombok (island) G5
Longiram F5
Lucipara Islands G7
Luwuk F6
Madiun G4
Madura (island) G4
Magelang G4
Mahakam (river) F5
Malikoor (island) G8
Majene F5
Makassar Strait E5, E6, F5

Malang G4
Malinau E5
Mamberamo (river) F9, F10
Mamuju F5
Manado E6
Mangole (island) F7
Manokwari F8
Manyu (islands) F9, F10
Mapia Islands E8
Maratua (island) E5
Martapura F4
Masalembo-Besar (island) G4
Mataboor F9
Mataram G5
Medan E1, m11
Mempawah E3
Mendawai (river) F4
Menggala F3
Mentawai Islands F1, F2
Merauke G10
Meulaboh m11
Misool (island) F7, F8
Molucca Passage F6
Molucca Sea E6, E7, F6, F7
Moluccas (islands) E7, F6, F7, F8, G7, G8
Monte Ramelau (mountain) G7
Morotai (island) E7
Muaratewe F4, F5
Muller Mountains E4, F4
Muntok F3
Musi (river) F2
Namlea F7
Natuna Besar (island) E3
Natuna Islands E3
Natuna Selatan (island) E3
New Guinea (island) F8, G8, G9, G10
Ngabang E3
Nias (island) E1, m11
Numfoor (island) F9
Obi Islands F7
Ogoamas (mountain) E6
Okaba G9
Pacific Ocean D7, D8, D9, E7, E8, E9, F7, F8, F9
Padang F2
Padangpanjang F2
Padangsidempuan E1, m11
Pagai Selatan (island) F2
Pagai Utara (island) F1, F2
Pagatan F4, G5
Pakanbaru F2
Palangkaraya F4
Palembang F2
Palopo F5
Pamekasan G4
Panaitan (island) G3
Pangkalanbuun F4
Pangkalpinang F3
Pantar (island) G6
Parepare F5
Parigi F6
Pasuruan G4

Pekalongan G3
Pelaihari F4
Pematangsiantar m11
Pembuang (river) F4
Perabumulih F2
Pini (island) E1
Piru F7
Point Lumut F3
Pontianak F3
Poso F6
Probolinggo G4
Quarles Mountains F4, F6
Raba G5
Rantekombola (mountain) F6
Rata (island) G2
Raya (mountain) F4
Riau Archipelago (islands) E2
Rinjani (peak) G5
Ruteng G6
Sanbang k11
Salawati (island) F8
Samarinda F5
Sambas E3
Samosir (island) E1, m11
Sampit F4
Sanana (island) F7
Sanggau E4
Sangihe (island) E7
Sarera Bay F8, F9
Saumlaki G8
Savu Sea G6
Sawahlunto F2
Schouten Islands F9
Schwaner Mountains F4
Selaru (island) G8
Seleyar (island) G6
Semarang G4
Semeru (mountain) G4
Semitau E4
Serang G3
Serua (island) G8
Serui F9
Siau (island) E7
Siberut (island) F1
Sibologa E1, m11
Sidikalang m11
Sigli k11
Simeulue (island) E4
Singapore E1, m11
Singapore (island) F2
Singaraja G5
Singkawang E3
Singkep (island) F2
Singkil E1, m11
Sintang E4
Sipura (island) F1
Slamet (mountain) G3
Sonsorol Islands E8
Sorong F8
Strait of Malacca E2
Sukabumi G6
Sukadana F3
Sukaraja F6
Sula Islands F5, F7

Sumatra (island) D1, E1, E2, F1, F2, F3, G2, G3, k11, m11
Sumba (island) G5, G6, H5, H6
Sumbawa (island) G5
Sumbawa Besar G5
Sumenep G4
Sunda Strait G3
Sungaiguntung E2
Sungaipenuh F2
Surabaya G4
Surakarta G4
Takole Kaju Mountains F5, F6
Talakmau (mountain) E1, E2
Talaud Islands E7
Taliabu (island) F6, F7
Tambelan Islands E3
Tanahbala (island) F1
Tanahgrogot F5
Tanahmasa (island) E1, F1
Tanimbar Islands G8
Tanjung F5
Tanjungbalai E1, m11
Tanjungkarang-Telukbetung F3
Tanjungpandan G3
Tanjungselor E5
Tapaktuan m11
Tarakan E5
Tasikmalaya G3
Tebingtinggi E1, m11
Tegal F8, F9
Tengah Islands G3
Tepa G5
Ternate E7
Ternate (island) E7
Tilamuta E6
Timor (island) G6, G7, H6
Timor Sea G7, H7
Toba (lake) E1, m11
Togian Islands E6
Tolitoli E6
Tondano E6
Trangan (island) G8
Trikora Peak (mountain) F9
Tual G8
Tukangbesi Islands G6
Tulungagung G4
Ujung Pandang G5
Upper Kapuas Mountains E4
Vaiiolo Passage E7, F7
Van Rees Mountains F9
Wahai F7
Waigeo (island) F8
Waikabubak G5
Waikelo G5
Waingapu G6
Waiwo E4
Waren F9
Watampone G5
Weda E7
Wetar (island) G7
Wokam (island) G8
Wowoni (island) F6
Yamdena (island) G8
Yogyakarta G4

MINI-FACTS AT A GLANCE

GENERAL INFORMATION

Official Name: Republic of Indonesia

Capital: Jakarta, on the island of Java

Government: Indonesia is a unitary multiparty republic with two legislative houses. The president, elected for a five-year term, is the head of the state and the government. A five-point statement of philosophy, *Pancasila*, sums up the national ideology; these are belief in one Supreme Being, humanitarianism, national unity, democracy by consensus, and social justice for all. *Golkar*, a group made up of professionals, military, and other special interest groups, is Indonesia's most powerful political organization.

The constitution provides for an elected Parliament and six branches of government: People's Consultative Assembly, Presidency, House of Representatives, Supreme Advisory Council, Supreme (or State) Audit Board, and the Supreme Court. Special religious courts handle Muslim family issues such as marriage and divorce. Administratively, the country is divided into 24 provinces, 1 metropolitan district of Jakarta Raya, and 2 special autonomous districts, Aceh and Yogyakarta.

Religion: The constitution supports monotheism—belief in one God—but guarantees religious freedom for all. The majority of the Indonesians (almost 90 percent) are Muslim, and believe in one God—Allah. Other people follow Christianity, Hinduism, and Buddhism. Hindus and Buddhists are concentrated on the island of Bali; 95 percent of the Balinese are Hindus.

Ethnic Composition: Indonesians represent hundreds of languages and cultural groups. Javanese, roughly 40 percent of the total population, are the largest ethnic group; Sundanese are the second largest with 15 percent. Other groups include Madurese, Balinese, Sasaks, Menadonese, Buginese, Dayaks, Irianese, and Ambonese. Some groups still rely on hunting and gathering to obtain food.

Language: Bahasa Indonesia is the official language; it is primarily derived from the Malay language with some Arabic, Dutch, Sanskrit, and English words. Almost everyone understands Bahasa Indonesia in addition to their own local dialect. More than 250 separate languages and dialects, belonging to the Malayo-Polynesian and Papuan families, are spoken with Javanese being the most widely used. English is the official second language of Indonesia. It is taught in secondary schools and used in industry.

National Flag: The red and white flag was originally used during the Majapahit Empire in the late 13th century. It was officially adopted as the national flag in 1949. The flag is horizontally divided into two equal parts: a red stripe at top signifying courage and a white stripe at bottom signifying purity.

National Emblem: Dating back to the 1200s, the national emblem consists of a shield with five symbols: a star (symbolizing God), a golden chain (humanity), a banyan tree (nationalism), a head of a buffalo (democracy), and rice and cotton (social justice). The shield hangs from the neck of an outstretched *Garuda* (the fierce man-eagle). The eagle carries a white scroll bearing the national motto in Bahasa Indonesia in black letters: *Bhinneka Tunggal Ika,* "Unity through Diversity."

National Anthem: *"Indonesia Raya"* ("Great Indonesia")

Money: The Indonesian rupiah (Rp) consists of 100 sen. In late 1993, 1 Indonesian rupiah was equal to $0.0005 in U.S. currency.

Membership in International Organizations: Association of Southeast Asian Nations (ASEAN); International Monetary Fund (IMF); Islamic Development Bank (IDB); Non-Aligned Movement (NAM); Organization of Petroleum Exporting Countries (OPEC); United Nations (UN), and others

Weights and Measures: The metric system is used.

Population: 198,070,000 (1994 estimate); the population density is 267 persons per sq. mi (103 persons per sq km); 30 percent urban and 70 percent rural. Indonesia is the fourth most populous nation in the world after China, India, and the United States. More than 60 percent of the total population lives in Java.

Cities:

City	Population
Jakarta	8,800,000
Surabaya	3,500,000
Medan	1,700,000
Bandung	1,400,000
Semarang	1,100,000

(Population figures based on 1987 estimates.)

GEOGRAPHY

Area: 741,101 sq. mi. (1,919,443 sq km)

Border: Indonesia is bounded on the north by the South China Sea, on the northeast by the Pacific Ocean, and on the south and west by the Indian Ocean. Land boundaries are shared with two countries, Malaysia and Papua New Guinea.

Indonesia is the third-largest country in Asia, and is the world's largest archipelago spreading over 17,500 islands; hundreds of these tiny islands are uninhabited.

Coastline: 34,000 mi. (54,716 km)

Land: Most of the islands are mountainous and lie on both sides of the equator. Indonesia with some 100 active volcanoes, is one of the most highly volcanic regions in the world. The nonacid lava has created good fertile soil.

Highest Point: Puncak Jaya, 16,500 ft. (5,029 m)

Lowest Point: Sea level along the coasts

Rivers: Most of its numerous rivers are short; some are navigable in parts. Mamberamo in Irian Jaya is the longest river.

Forests and Flora: Some 75 percent of the total land area is forested. About 10 percent of all plant species in the world can be found in Indonesia and about 10 percent of the world's rain forests are found here. Flora includes palms, ferns, bamboo, chestnuts, oak, vines, mosses, rattan, spice trees (cloves, nutmeg), fruit trees, aromatic camphor, sandalwood, and hardwood trees such as teak and ebony. Mangrove forests flourish in tidal areas of the islands. Indonesia is the world's largest exporter of wood. With extensive logging and little replanting the rain forests are disappearing at a fast rate. Indonesia bans the export of raw logs in favor of creating domestic wood-using industries. More than 2,500 species of wild orchids are found in Irian Jaya only. *Rafflesia*, the world's largest flower (about 39 in. [1 m] in diameter) grows in Sumatra.

Wildlife: A number of exotic animals live in Indonesia's forests and water. Some 500 types of animals including tigers, rhinoceroses, lions, elephants, wild pigs, tapirs, orangutans, and leopards inhabit the forests. The Komodo dragon lizard is one of the rarest in the world and is found only on the island of Komodo; it can grow to a length of 10 ft. (3 m). Other rare animals are the bandicoot (a marsupial) and the Sulawesian anoa (a dwarf buffalo). Indonesian wildlife is preserved in more than 300 nature reserves, protected forests, and national parks.
There are some 1,500 species of birds on the islands including parrots, mynahs, cockatoos, cassowaries, and birds of paradise. Crocodiles, giant sea turtles, dolphins, and numerous kinds of fish and coral abound in the seas. Ornamental tropical fish are an important export item.

Climate: The tropical climate has heavy rainfall, high temperatures, and high humidity throughout the year. At sea level temperatures range from 78° to 90° F. (25° to 32° C). The highest mountains are cold enough to keep a snow cover year around. The humidity averages 80 percent throughout the year. The wet season is from November to March and the dry season from June to October. Several inches of rain falls nearly every month on most of the islands.

Greatest Distance: East to West: 3,275 mi. (5,271 km)
North to South: 1,373 mi. (2,210 km)

ECONOMY AND INDUSTRY

Agriculture: Indonesia ranks among the largest rice producers in the world. Most of the rice is grown in Java. Rubber is the chief cash crop. Sago, yams, taro, bananas, cassava, coconut and copra, corn, sweet potatoes, and spices (cloves, nutmeg, mace) are the chief crops. Export crops such as sugarcane, rubber, tobacco, palm, coffee, tea, cocoa, and cinchona are raised on large plantations. Food crops are raised on small family farms. Rich volcanic soil, heavy rains, and plenty of sunshine have made Java and Bali two of the most fertile tropical islands in the world. Slash-and-burn agriculture is still practiced in remote areas. Livestock includes goats, cattle, sheep, hogs, chicken, and water buffalo.

Fishing is a very important aspect of the Indonesian economy. The farmers raise fish and eel in the flooded rice fields. A variety of fish are caught including prawns, anchovies, mackerel, sardines, and tuna. Fish is the main source of protein in the Indonesian diet.

Mining: Indonesia is one of the largest producers of petroleum in Asia and is the world's second-largest producer of tin. The country is the world's leading exporter of liquefied natural gas. Other minerals include coal, nickel, bauxite, copper, and iron ore. Some gold and silver are also mined.

Manufacturing: The chief manufacturing items include refined petroleum and petroleum by-products, automobiles and trucks, machinery and machine tools, aircraft, glassware, processed foods, textiles, cement, chemicals, fertilizer, paper, tires, soap, and cigarettes.

Transportation: Dense forests and mountainous terrain are the major obstacles in the development of transportation. In the late 1980s there were some 4,088 mi. (6,580 km) of railway lines, almost all owned by the government; road length was 74,257 mi. (119,500 km). Indonesian merchant marines consist of some 2,000 vessels. Several local ferry companies carry people along the coasts and between islands. Government-owned Garuda Indonesia Airline is the national airline. Merpati Nusantara Airline operates most of the domestic jet services. Jakarta is the chief international airport; there are some 120 airports in Indonesia. Tanjungpriok, near Jakarta, is the chief seaport.

Communication: The postal, telegraph, and telephone systems are owned by the government. The government also owns the radio and television services. *Asian*

Wall Street Journal and *International Herald Tribune* are the two largest international papers available. There are more than 60 daily and 100 weekly newspapers published in Bahasa Indonesia or other local languages. The government has established strict press guidelines over the years.

Trade: Indonesia is a free trade leader in Southeast Asia. The major imports are machinery, transport equipment, chemicals, and raw minerals. The major import sources are Japan, United States, and Germany. The chief exports are crude petroleum, natural gas, plywood, garments, and rubber. Chief export destinations are Japan, United States, and Singapore.

EVERYDAY LIFE

Health: Major diseases include tuberculosis, malaria, dysentery, rabies, cholera, and plague.

Education: Since 1945 the government has introduced many special programs to increase literacy. Now some two-thirds of the population can read and write. The educational system consists of six years in primary school, three years in middle school, and three years in high school. Elementary education is free and compulsory for six years; secondary education is not compulsory. Regional languages may be used to teach until the third grade, but after that all education is given in Bahasa Indonesia. Most of the schools are coeducational; students normally wear uniforms. There are many specialized vocational schools and some 50 public and private universities for higher education. The University of Indonesia at Jakarta and the University of Gajah Mada at Yogyakarta are the two best-known institutions of higher learning.

Holidays:

> New Year's Day, January 1
> Indonesian National Day, August 17
> Christmas, December 25

Movable religious holidays include the Prophet's Birthday, Ascension of Muhammad, Good Friday, the end of Ramadan, and the 1st of Muharram (Muslim New Year).

Culture: Many Indonesians, like Sukarno and Soeharto, have only one given name, as is the tradition in Java. Family and village ties are very strong. Many village decisions are made by the elders. Extended families live, work, and play together.

Balinese dances often are based on the ancient Hindu epic *Ramayan*. Puppet plays are an integral part of the Javanese and Balinese culture. The *gamelan* orchestra consists of percussion instruments ranging from five to 50; this instrumental ensemble has been around for hundreds of years. Many different kinds (leather, paper, wood) of puppets are used; Java's shadow-puppet theater is one of a kind.

Batik, the art of waxing and dying cloth into beautiful patterns and colors, is the most famous Indonesian craft. *Ikat* is a method of weaving, somewhat like tie-dyeing. Indonesian artists are involved in weaving and designing textiles, carving, sculpturing, making puppets and craft items, performing puppet shows, dancing, and playing in orchestras. The Central Museum in Jakarta has displays of Indonesian history and culture; the Zoological Museum is at Bogor, Java. The restored Borobudur Temple complex at Bali, the largest Buddhist temple in the world, is a major tourist destination.

Clothing: Indonesian men and women wear a kind of colorful skirt called a *sarong* that is wrapped around the body. Men wear a shirt and women wear a long-sleeved blouse with the *sarong*. People wear Western-style clothes in the cities. Women wear a scarflike cloth over the shoulders and on the head. Men wear a special hat or cap.

Housing: Housing is a problem both in urban and rural areas. Most of the rural houses have no electricity or running water. Rural dwellings consist of a sleeping room and a large living room. A clay oven in the living room is used for cooking; fish and meat are dried and smoked over this oven. Traditional rural houses are built on stilts; the space underneath is used for livestock and poultry. In Java most of the houses are built on the ground. Occasional longhouses still exist in some villages, where about 100 people live under the same roof.

Food: Rice is the staple of the western Indonesian diet; sago or yam are staples in other regions. Rice is eaten boiled or fried and is served with many other special dishes of meat, fish, vegetables, or chicken. Eating pork is forbidden by Islam. Sumatran food is hot and spicy while Javanese dishes are milder. Indian curries and Chinese dishes are popular. *Martabak*, a kind of pancake; *sate*, skewered meat in peanut sauce; and noodles are available in *warung*, fast-food stalls. Food is sometimes served wrapped in banana or coconut leaves. Tea and coffee are the most common beverages.

Sports and Recreation: Badminton, basketball, tennis, and soccer are the most popular games. Bicycling, swimming, and volleyball are also popular. Children enjoy kite flying. *Taman Mini Indonesia Indah*, a large theme park outside Jakarta, is visited by thousands of Indonesians everyday.

Social Welfare: Only a small percent (roughly 10 percent) of the population benefits from a state insurance scheme. Benefits include life insurance and old-age pensions.

IMPORTANT DATES

2500-500 B.C.—People migrate to Indonesia from the Asian mainland

A.D. 600-1,200—The Buddhist kingdom of Srivijaya becomes a great sea power

750-850—Buddhist kingdom called Sailendra flourishes in central Java

1292—Marco Polo visits the Indonesian island of Sumatra

1300s—The Hindu kingdom of Majapahit controls most of Indonesia

1343—Javanese armies of the Majapahit dynasty attack the island of Bali

1377—Javanese Majapahit attacks Srivijaya kingdom

1400s—Islam starts spreading on the islands

1497-98—Portuguese explorer Vasco da Gama sails around Africa

1500s—Portuguese control most of the Indonesian island trade

1511—Portuguese capture Malacca on the Malay Peninsula

1527—Troops of the Sultan of Demak attack and conquer the capital of the west Java kingdom

1596—The first Dutch ships land in Banten

1600s—Christianity is introduced by Portuguese and Spanish traders

1602—A group of Dutch traders form the Dutch East India Company

1614—Jan Pieterszoon Coen is put in charge of Dutch East India Company's operations

1620s—The Dutch start to control most of the islands

1641—Dutch capture Malacca Island from the Portuguese

1778—The Central Museum Library, the oldest in Indonesia, is established in Jakarta

1795—France invades Holland

1798 — Dutch East India Company is dissolved

1799 — The Dutch government takes over the land controlled by the Dutch East India Company

1811-1816 — British forces control the Dutch East Indies during the Napoleonic Wars in Europe

1814 — The Central Library of Biological Sciences and Agriculture is established in Java

1815 — Mt. Krakatau erupts, killing thousands of people on the nearby islands. French emperor Napoleon Bonaparte is defeated

1816 — The Dutch government starts ruling Indonesia once again

1825 — A Javanese prince launches a guerrilla war against the Dutch colonial government

1830 — Dutch government forces Indonesian farmers to grow indigo and coffee on most of their farms

1870 — Dutch investors are permitted to lease farmland on Indonesian islands

1883 — Mt. Krakatau erupts once again; some thirty-five thousand people are killed by accompanying massive tidal waves on nearby islands

1890 — Java Man fossils are discovered on the island of Java

1908 — Indonesians begin to form nationalist groups; *Budi Utomo,* "noble conduct," is Indonesia's first significant nationalist organization

1916 — *Sarekat Islam,* a Muslim political party, holds its first convention

1927 — Some nationalist leaders take part in the "League Against Imperialism and Colonial Oppression" in Brussels; Sukarno founds the Indonesian National party

1928 — The second Youth Congress is held in Jakarta. The first Indonesia Women's Congress is held in Yogyakarta; Bahasa Indonesia is used for the first time as an official language at this meeting

1933-42 — Sukarno and Muhammad Hatta are held in custody by the Dutch government

1940—German troops invade the Netherlands

1942—Japanese forces occupy Indonesia; end of the Dutch rule in Indonesia

1945—Japanese forces leave Indonesia; Sukarno and Muhammad Hatta proclaim Indonesia independent; Sukarno becomes the first president and Hatta becomes the first vice-president of independent Indonesia

1949—The Dutch recognize Indonesia's independence; the Federal Republic of the United States of Indonesia is established; Sukarno is elected the first president

1950—Indonesia becomes a unitary state; it is the 60th country to join the United Nations; Dutch still control Irian Jaya and Portuguese control East Timor

1953—Indonesian Central Bank is established

1954—Indonesia ends union with the Netherlands

1955—Afro-Asian conference is held at Bandung; first national elections are held

1956—Sukarno introduces concept of "guided democracy"

1957—Sukarno declares state of war

1958—Indonesia cuts off all trade with the Netherlands and expels all Dutch people still living in the islands

1959—Sukarno gains great political power; appoints himself president and begins his program of "guided democracy;" Sukarno reinstates by decree the constitution of 1945. Dutch plantations are seized and nationalized

1960—All political parties are banned

1961—Non-Aligned Movement is formed by 29 developing nations

1962—Television is introduced; Sukarno escapes two assassination attempts

1963—Sukarno is named president for life; West New Guinea (now Irian Jaya) comes under Indonesian control

1965—A revolt led by army officers accused of being Communists is crushed by General Soeharto. Sukarno nationalizes several oil companies and rubber plantations. Indonesia withdraws from the UN

1966—Soeharto takes over much of Sukarno's power; he reorganizes the government; Indonesian membership in the UN is restored; anti-Communist purges take place with 100,000 reported killed

1967—Indonesia joins Association of Southeast Asian Nations (ASEAN) as charter member; Sukarno is stripped of all powers and titles and is barred from presidential palace; Soeharto is named acting president

1968—Soeharto is elected president

1969—Voters in West Irian Jaya agree to a union with Indonesia

1970—Sukarno dies; judiciary is made independent; Soeharto visits the Netherlands

1971—Second parliamentary elections are held

1972—Pertamina, the state petroleum organization, is formed

1973—Soeharto is elected president for a second five-year term

1975—Portuguese abruptly leave East Timor; Indonesian military forces invade and incorporate East Timor into Indonesia, some 200,000 people die in struggle; East Timor is declared a province of Indonesia

1978—Soeharto is reelected president for a third term

1983—Guerrilla movements escalate in Timor and Irian Jaya with government establishing various repressive measures

1986—Oil revenues drop dramatically and development projects are affected

1988—Indonesia officially recognizes the state of Palestine

1990—Demands for greater democracy and Soeharto's retirement are voiced throughout Indonesia; military force is used to put down a rebellion in northern Sumatra. A border agreement is signed with Papua New Guinea

1991—At least one hundred mourners are massacred by Indonesian soldiers in East Timor

1992—Indonesia hosts the tenth NAM Summit Conference in Jakarta; it is attended by its 100-member nations and 19 observer nations. Indonesia passes a law allowing selected foreign businesses to start up with 100 percent foreign ownership.

1993—A super tanker carrying 78 million gallons of crude oil collides with another ship in the Strait of Malacca between Sumatra island and Malaysia; Soeharto is unanimously reelected by the People's Consultative Assembly for another 5-year term

1994—An earthquake measuring between 6.5 and 7.2 on the Richter scale occurs in the southern part of Sumatra, killing more than 134 people and causing extensive damage to homes, buildings, and roads

IMPORTANT PEOPLE

Jan Pieterszoon Coen (1858-1929), an ambitious Dutch trader who extended Dutch power in the East Indies

Eugene Dubois (1858-1940), Dutch scientist, anatomist, and paleontologist; he discovered fossils of a primitive form of human who lived about half a million years ago; he named it in 1891 as *Pithecanthropus erectus*, also known as Java Man

Vasco da Gama (1460-1524), Portuguese explorer and navigator who sailed around the Cape of Good Hope

Dr. Muhammad Hatta (1902-1980), a nationalist leader; served as Sukarno's first vice-president and prime minister

Cornelis de Houtman (c.1540-1599), Dutch captain who brought the first Dutch sailors to Java

Jayabaya of Kediri (12th century), ruler of a Javanese kingdom; wrote a book of prophesies

Princess Raden Ajeng Kartini (1879-1904), founder of a school for girls; led a movement for the equal rights for women

Kublai Khan (1215-1294), founder of Mongol dynasty in China; grandson of Genghis Khan; he conquered Burma, Cambodia, and other parts of southeast Asia; turned back by Java

Adam Malik (1917-1984), foreign minister (1966-1977); vice-president (1978-1983); an international negotiator; restored and improved relations with Malaysia, the Philippines, the United Kingdom, the United States, and the United Nations

Jawaharlal Nehru (1889-1964), a nationalist leader and prime minister of India from 1947 to 1964; cofounder of Non-Aligned Movement (NAM)

Marco Polo (1254-1324), a Venetian traveler and merchant; he was one of the first writers to tell the world about the Far East

Ptolemy (2nd century), noted geographer, astronomer, mathematician, and writer who lived in Alexandria, Egypt, and described Java in his writings

Sir Thomas Stanford Raffles (1781-1826), British lieutenant governor-general of Java

General Soeharto (1921-   ), leader of Indonesia since Sukarno's overthrow in 1968; reelected president in 1973, 1978, 1983, 1988, and 1993

Dr. Sukarno (1901-1970), founder and leader of the nationalist movement; first president of independent Indonesia

Pramoedya Ananta Toer, Indonesian writer; imprisoned after 1965 riots; writings include *This Earth of Mankind*

Umar Wirahadikusumah (1924-   ), a retired army general; became vice-president in 1983

INDEX

Page numbers that appear in boldface type indicate illustrations

Snorkeling in the clear waters near the coral reefs

About the Author

Sylvia McNair is the author of more than a dozen books for adults and young people about interesting places, including *Enchantment of the World: India.* Her articles on travel appear regularly in national magazines. A graduate of Oberlin College, she has toured all fifty of the United States, as well as more than thirty-five countries on six continents. She was born in Korea and says that Asian countries are especially fascinating to her. "The Far East is getting closer to us all the time," she says. "We need to learn more about these ancient civilizations."

Regarding her research for this book, Mrs. McNair says, "My sincere thanks go to Garuda Indonesia Airline, the Indonesian Directorate of Tourism, and Patricia Lewis, for their help in my research."

Sylvia McNair lives in Evanston, Illinois. She has three sons, one daughter, and two grandsons.